Narrative Therapy and Community Work:
A conference collection

Narrative Therapy and Community Work:

A conference collection

from Dulwich Centre Publications

Copyright © 1999 *by* Dulwich Centre Publications
ISBN 0 9586678 8 8

published by
Dulwich Centre Publications
Hutt St PO Box 7192
Adelaide, South Australia 5000
phone (61-8) 8223 3966 fax (61-8) 8232 4441

printed & manufactured in Australia by:
Graphic Print Group, Richmond, South Australia

100% recycled
paper

cover artwork by: Danni McLean, South Australia
cover design by: Norm Golding, typegraphics, South Australia
typeset, layout & design by: Jane Hales, South Australia

Contents

Day Three

Reflections

Appendix: Related reading

Farewell from Adelaide *(song)*

Introduction

Welcome to this collection of papers from the inaugural Dulwich Centre Publications' Narrative Therapy and Community Work Conference. We hope you enjoy reading the wide range of writings within these pages. They seem to us to convey much of the spirit that pervaded the conference.

As well as publishing a range of presentations that took place at the conference, we have included here excerpts from the daily conference newspaper, the lyrics of the welcome and farewell song, and a small number of reflections from participants.

There was so much material that it was impossible to include all of the presentations that occurred at the conference. To make up for this, we have included a list of references at the back of the book to indicate where people can read more about particular presentations that are not included here. Other presentations will be published in upcoming editions of *Gecko*.

After the good response to our first conference, we are now planning our next one for February 2000. We had always envisaged having another conference - utilising the learnings of the first in the second! The dates are now confirmed for next year. There will be a week of events from Sunday 13 February to Saturday 19 February. The conference itself will run for three days (16-18 February). For more information about next year's conference and pre- and post-conference events, please see p.214 of this book, or our web page: dulwichcentre.com.au

We hope you enjoy reading this collection. Perhaps we'll see you in Adelaide in February 2000!

The Conference Collective

Day One

Welcome to the land

by

Lewis O'Brien

Senior Elder of the Kaurna People

Munara, ngai wanggandi 'Marni na Budni Kaurna yertaanna'.
Worttangga, 'Marni na budni Banba-banbalya'.
Ngai Birko-mankolankola Tandanyanku.

First let me welcome you all to Kaurna Country.
Next, 'I welcome you all to the Conference',
as Ambassador of the Adelaide people.

I used the word *Banba-banbalya* which means conference. Our people ran conferences in this country for thousands of years.

I have an Uncle on tape telling how the Narrunga, Ngadjuri, Nukunu and the Kaurna came together. You might say, 'So what?' Then I might put this to you: in Australia there were 250 Aboriginal languages and 850 dialects, and yet all the different groups had the Dreaming. That to me shows a management educational achievement that has not been done anywhere else in the world.

Ngaityo Yungandalya Ngaityo Yakkanandalya

Thank you my brothers, my sisters.

1

A welcome note

from the

Conference Collective

Welcome to Adelaide '99 - our first conference!

For many, many months we have been awaiting this morning with a sense of delight and anticipation. We had originally imagined a conference of 300 participants. This morning we welcome twice that number. It means a great deal to us that many participants have travelled long distances to be here and have left friends and family for a significant period of time. We wish to acknowledge the effort that people have made to come - especially those who have travelled from winter to summer.

We also wish to acknowledge the work of presenters, many of whom have been busily rehearsing their presentations for months now. We especially want to highlight the efforts that have occurred behind the scenes that have ensured that so many presentations during this conference will be presentations in partnership. We believe that this will invite conversations into territories that otherwise would not have been possible.

For many years, Dulwich Centre Publications has tried to create a forum of the written word for community conversations over a range of issues. It is a new step to try to bring these readers and writers together in the same place to have the conversations in person! This is the first conference we have organised. We are very excited about the possibilities this new direction opens up, and we are also sure that we have much to learn. We are thinking of organising a second conference in the year 2000. If people have ideas as to what might contribute to this second conference please let us know - either in person or in writing. Our suggestion box is in the Publications room.

For this conference, we have tried to create a venue which will sustain a diversity of conversations - from informal discussions under trees, to 'intense' tent sessions, to more formal skills-based workshops in lecture theatres. To do this we have gambled on the February weather being kind. By Friday we'll know if the gamble paid off! We have also tried to create a program of presentations from a diversity of perspectives and we are particularly excited about how this has come together.

Over these three days we'd like to invite everyone who is gathered here into considerations of care-taking. The issues that will be discussed this week include some of our most heartfelt and profound struggles. We would like to encourage people to think through what good self-care would look like over the time of this conference. We have deliberately chosen the venue so that it is very easy to simply take time off and sit under a tree or take a stroll by the river. It is not expected that participants will attend all of the sessions; in fact we strongly recommend that people take time to relax, rest and ground themselves between the sessions they do attend. During the conference, if you need to speak with someone at any time in relation to care-taking, please feel free to approach any person wearing a blue name-badge.

We'd also like to invite participants into considerations of care for presenters. For some sessions we have deliberately limited the number of participants as the topics being discussed require great care and thoughtfulness. We'd ask you to please attend the sessions for which you have received confirmation and which are indicated on your name-badge. Considerable thought and energy has gone into deciding the numbers for each presentation. Thank you.

After three days of thoughtful conversation and the sharing of stories, we reckon that it will be time for a celebration! Our hope is that WOMADelaide, which begins on Friday evening straight after the conference, will be an opportunity to 'let down our hair', dance and sing.

After many months of planning and anticipation, the inaugural Dulwich Centre Publications conference begins! We'd like to welcome you to Adelaide '99. Thank you for coming.

Welcome song

Chorus:
> Welcome to Adelaide
> to this conference
> gathering over these three days
> If you're new to Australia
> Well G'day and how are ya?
> If you're a local, well good on ya
> and welcome anyway!

Making new connections
Making new friends
we wish this all for you
as this conference begins

There've been an awful lot of
preparations
people have come from many nations
Over these three days
please take good care
come Friday night and
WOMADelaide
then we'll let down our hair!

Chorus:
> Welcome to Adelaide
> to this conference
> gathering over these three days

If you're new to Australia
Well G'day and how are ya?
If you're a local, well good on ya
and welcome anyway!

Welcome to this conference
hope you're ready to enjoy
the richness of experience
that surrounds us all

Hopefully you'll find what you've
come for
From skills-based workshops
to meeting friends from afar
We're so glad you came
Next year, if all goes well
perhaps we'll do it all again!

Chorus:
> Welcome to Adelaide
> to this conference
> gathering over these three days
> If you're new to Australia
> Well G'day and how are ya?
> If you're a local, well good on ya
> and welcome anyway!

1.

Telling our stories in ways that make us stronger

by

Barb Wingard[1]

As Indigenous people of this country, we have faced so many losses due to past and present injustice. Grief's presence has been with us for a long time. Now we are seeking ways of speaking about Grief that are consistent with our cultural ways of doing things. We are remembering those who have died, we are honouring Indigenous spiritual ways, and we are finding ways of grieving that bring us together. We are telling our stories in ways that make us stronger.

Dealing with our grief, with all of the losses we have experienced, is not about moving on and forgetting. It's about remembering our people and bringing them with us wherever we go.

I've lost a brother, my father, my grandmother too, but I believe that they're still with me. I carry a lot of their ways. I acknowledge them.

We Aboriginal people have had too many losses. Sometimes it seems as if we are moving from one death to another. Our people just get so weary; at times it's too much to go to one more funeral.

We simply have to find ways of grieving together because it's far too hard to do it on our own.

I remember talking to a young Aboriginal man in Murray Bridge late last year. There have been so many deaths in his family and recently he's been diagnosed as having a mental illness. I met up with him because the mental health team had said, 'Would you like to see Auntie Barb to talk about some of these things?'

We sat out on the lawn and made our first connection. We didn't call it counselling, we just called it talking together under the trees. He began to share stories with me about so many deaths - all his uncles have died, and his father - there's been one after the other. He spoke of how he believes his illness has come because of the grief.

The environment and the way that we were sitting made it comfortable for him to talk. As he spoke about all the people who have passed on, we acknowledged them quietly.

He's a brilliant young lad. He's finished year 12 and has got big plans about having his own business. He showed me how he's going to do this in stages. He also showed me a memorial he's been working on, for all those who have passed away. He's acknowledged special things about each individual. He's found meaning for each one and he's painting them each a different image. It is a beautiful memorial. He's looking at a lot of the cultural aspects of their lives as well - reflecting on all that has happened in this land, and how a lot of the problems nowadays relate to what happened in the past.

These days, if you talk too much about the past, people look at you as a radical - they think you're trying to stir up trouble There are those who say, 'We've got to forget about the past and move on'. That's fine to a point, but I think we have to acknowledge the events that happened in the past that had an impact on our grandparents, our parents, and, whether we acknowledge it or not, on ourselves. When people say, 'Forget the past', they're asking us to leave a lot behind. They're asking us to desert our old folks. We cannot move on and leave them behind - we must bring them with us wherever we go.

A part of Aboriginal people's story-telling is that we hold onto our loved ones who aren't here any longer. Our old people are who we belong to. Through them we identify each other. When an Aboriginal person meets another Aboriginal person, we work out how we know each other through our relatives. I might not know your parents, but who were their parents? We constantly reflect and remember these people.

All *my* histories are through my grandmother. Everybody knows of her and her children. Hanging on to these old people is very much part of our strength. It is part of our story-telling. They are talked about so much that they are still with us.

When a people has had as many losses as we have had, it is not time to forget and move on. It is time to remember, to stay connected to our people, past and present. We will not forget our people and we will not forget the past. We have to acknowledge and keep on acknowledging all that has happened in this country.

Thirty-five years ago I was fifteen and it was 1964. In those days there was an Aborigines Act where some Aboriginal people were given an Exemption which allowed us to mix with the wider community, but it also indicated that we ceased to be Aboriginal.

This act prevented many of my people from returning to their birth places on the missions. There was also a loitering act which prevented people of different races congregating together. This included mixing with our own people as well as our white friends. In those days, we were not even citizens of this country. That didn't happen until 1967.

So many of our losses have been unjust, and this is what is so hard to deal with. We are losing a lot of our people well before their time. Many of our deaths are not natural - for example, deaths in custody. It is tragic that we are losing our people so young.

When my father died he was thirty-nine, a week off his fortieth birthday. To us that is a tragic event, but it is a common one. People like me, who are in our fifties, we count our blessings that we are here each day. We say to each other how lucky we are to still be alive. We don't take life for granted.

It's important for us as Aboriginal people to make the links between justice and grief. We need the injustices addressed so that we can grieve our losses. We need our stories told and acknowledged. Working on our grief in these ways is working towards justice.

Aboriginal people have many different ways of dealing with grief. Often when people die there can be a good feeling that their spirit will be going to meet with all the other spirits, other lost loved ones. A lot of Aboriginal people also experience signs from loved ones who have passed away. Seeing particular birds, for example, is often experienced as having ongoing contact with people who have died, ongoing contact with their spirits.

We are trying to listen to people's stories to put them more in touch with their own healing ways.

My father died when I was 14, and I remember seeing him in the coffin. I wanted to cry loud and yet the environment that we were in didn't allow for me to grieve in my way. I think European society has encouraged particular ways of grieving and they don't necessarily fit for Aboriginal people. If you go to a funeral service in an Aboriginal community you can wail and cry and grieve the way you want to grieve. But in mainstream funeral services there seems to be a lot of silence to grieving.

I don't believe that this silence fits with Aboriginal culture. I don't believe that this silence is a good thing. I especially don't think it's good for our young men. Some of the women perhaps have a better mechanism because they have a network in which they're not afraid to shed tears. But silent cries can go on for years and be heard by no-one. They can eat away at a person's spirit.

If only all those people who are silently crying could find ways to come together. I think they'd be quite amazed how much they have in common and how much they'd want to share somebody else's story.

We are trying to find ways to bring together our people who are grieving. Camp Coorong, in 1994, was one attempt in which all Aboriginal families in South Australia who had experienced a death in custody gathered together. The document that came from this gathering was called 'Reclaiming Our Stories, Reclaiming Our Lives' (1995).

Here is an extract from it:

Aboriginal people have always had their own special ways of healing. This includes ways of healing the pain from loss and injustice.

These healing ways have been disrespected by non-Aboriginal people, and Aboriginal people have been discouraged from using them. But the healing ways have survived and are playing an important part in Aboriginal life today.

Talking together more about the healing ways is one path to taking them back, to making them stronger. (p.15)

Another aspect of the gathering was to find special ways of remembering - ways of remembering that make it possible for people to see themselves through the eyes of the lost loved one.

Recently, I remember speaking to a man who was very angry with his Dad who had died years ago. Gradually we brought his father to our conversations, let him join us, and over time he remembered his father putting his arms around him. There were so many stories that had been forgotten.

As this man gradually saw himself through the eyes of his father, he reconnected with his father's love. As he told the stories of this love, I watched a weight lift from him. It was almost like Mr Anger just jumped out of his body and I was looking at a different person. His expression was so soft as he spoke of wanting to share these stories of his father with his brothers and his sisters. I don't know where Mr Anger went, but it was beautiful to watch him go.

When we reclaim the stories we want to tell about our lives, when we reconnect with those we have lost, and the memories we have forgotten, then we become stronger.

Not only are we telling our stories differently, but we are listening differently too. We are listening for our people's abilities and knowledges and skills. We've been knocked so many times that we often don't think very well of ourselves. But we're finding ways to acknowledge one another and to see the abilities that people have but may not know they have. Without putting people on pedestals, we are finding ways of acknowledging each others' stories of survival.

Talking with Grief

We are also looking for healing ways of talking about our losses. One way is to externalise Grief. At times I play the character of Grief and invite others to ask me questions:

- *What is your name?*
- *Have we met you before?*
- *Has your presence been with Aboriginal people for a long time?*
- *How have we dealt with you in the past?*
- *How can we deal with you now?*

In this way we begin to talk about the journey of Aboriginal history. We speak of the loss of land, sickness, deaths, the stolen generation, the loss of language -

as well as the ways in which Aboriginal people have responded.

For Aboriginal people, in some ways, inviting people into conversations with Grief is encouraging people to hold on. Grief invites us to cherish our people and our histories. We need to take up its invitations.

We need to talk about our history with our own people. I think the young children that we have now, the youth, really need to know our stories, including our stories of loss and how we have dealt with them. In some ways this is honouring of our grief.

I think that the words 'death', 'they've gone', 'I'll never see them', leave a lot of people feeling bad about death. Death and grief are very scary for some people. But one day we too are going to pass away and join the spirits.

As Indigenous people of this country, our stories are precious. They have survived over generations. Our elderly have passed them on to us and we will continue to pass them to our children. As Indigenous Australians we're going to keep telling our stories in ways that make us stronger.

Note

1. Barb can be contacted c/- Murray Mallee Community Health, PO Box 346, Murray Bridge 5253, South Australia, phone (61-8) 8535 6800.

Reference

Aboriginal Health Council of South Australia, 1995: 'Reclaiming Our Stories, Reclaiming Our Lives.' *Dulwich Centre Newsletter*, 1.

2.

The politics of illness narratives:

Who tells, who listens and who cares?

by

Kathy Weingarten[1]

Still reeling from the scene that had played out in the natural world, I moved inside to the workshop space, a wood-paneled amphitheatre. I had awakened that day to a light misty rain, an occurrence I hadn't thought possible in hot, dry Adelaide in February. Arriving at the conference venue, I could tell there was some consternation about whether the opening ceremony would need to be moved inside, even though all the arrangements were in place on the lawns.

Barb Wingard, a Nunga woman from Murray Bridge who was to be the keynote speaker, assured the Conference Collective that the weather would co-operate, and indeed it did. She gave her stirring opening address, there was a performance by an Indigenous Australian dance troupe, a few short announcements and then, blam, the rain came pouring down.

My western mind had no way of understanding the timing of the rain. Walking up the five flights of stairs to the amphitheatre, I wondered how many people coming to the workshop on illness narratives would bring a western mind and how many a mind shaped by other, non-western influences? The rain/no rain event was auspicious. It raised the same question for me in the natural world that I wished to consider in the human realm. How do our ways of knowing influence the narratives we tell?

In my presentation, I focused on illness narratives, exploring ways we give meaning to our illnesses; ways we tell an illness narrative; the range of effects different kinds of illness narratives have; and the implications of this for caring for those who are ill or disabled. Although I have been writing about illness narratives for a decade, and speaking to large audiences about them for half that time, this was the first time I had made culture a primary filter for conceptualising the development of and interpretation of illness narratives.

By ten after the hour, one hundred or so participants were in the room. Ireni Esler, a social worker from New Zealand, gave a lovely personal introduction to my work, trying to interest people in it and make them at ease. I tried to continue in her vein:

Good morning. How is this space for you? Are you comfortable? We cannot be outdoors, but the Conference Collective has given us these two huge flower arrangements to feast our eyes on. Please feel free to leave at any time you may need to, to move around, and to stretch ... I am going to do the best I can to make eye contact with you, but the lights are directly in my eyes and it is hard for me to see. I hope you will understand ...

I spend time in the beginning of these workshops on illness narratives inviting people's embodied selves into the room and sharing my embodied self. The dominant discourse of workshops and conferences is that we are minds-in-space; no official recognition is given to our corporeal reality.[2] Many who attend my workshops are people for whom the body and its ills have been marginalised in painful ways, as hurtful as the discomfort the body's ills produce. I want to actively oppose, not replicate, those practices of marginalisation.

Another way I oppose the marginalisation of the body is to situate myself as a person who has been drawn to this topic because of my own illness journey. In doing so, I oppose another dominant cultural message, one that 'asserts' that professionals should separate the personal and the professional. For me the personal is the professional and vice versa.

I am the daughter of a mother who died of cancer, a woman who has had breast cancer twice, and the mother of a daughter who was born with a rare genetic disorder and who 'came out' as a person with disabilities in 1996. These experiences have shaped who I am and what I bring to my professional life as surely as anything else has done so.

Finally, in setting the scene for my presentation, I honour my mother and my daughter. My mother, Violet Weingarten, wrote about her illness experience in 1975; her book, *Intimations of Mortality*, was published posthumously.[3] My daughter, Miranda Eve Weingarten Worthen, has written about these issues with me and given me permission to speak about her.[4] The courage of these women envelops me; their insistence on voice inspires me.

Questions

I ask people to do personal work with each other on their own illness narratives or the illness narratives of someone they know well. It is asking a lot of people to launch into such personal subjects. One way I help people in the audience feel comfortable talking to strangers is to ground the theoretical concepts I present in my family's illness narrative. Another way is by asking questions of the audience about illness and disability so that people can see the range of illness experience shared by those who are in the room:

Just to get an idea of the experiences of the people in the room regarding illness and family illness, I will ask a series of questions. I am referring to what is described traditionally as physical and mental illness. Please feel free not to raise your hand if to do so would require you to reveal more about yourself or your family and friends than you are comfortable doing.

1. *How many of you have ever been ill for more than one month?*
   As a child? As a teenager? As an adult?

2. *How many of you have lived with a person who has had an illness of more than one month's duration?*
   As a child? As a teenager? As an adult?

3. *How many of you have been the primary caretaker of a person with an illness of more than one month's duration?*

4. *How many of you have lived with a person who had a disability -*
   physical, emotional or mental - that impaired some aspect of his or her
   functioning?

   > *As a child? As a teenager? As an adult?*

5. *How many of you have ever found it difficult to talk with other family*
   members, friends or acquaintances about the experiences you have had
   as an ill person or about the experiences you have had caring for an ill
   person?

6. *How often do you think people associate the words strong and*
   independent with an ill or disabled person? Very common? Some of the
   time? Rarely?

7. *Thinking back to your own experiences with illness - even the flu will do*
   - how many of you struggled with the temporary feelings of dependence
   or weakness?

These questions orient us to our own experience and to the experiences of those
of us who have had illnesses and to those of us who have cared for persons with
illnesses.

The politics of illness narratives

The heart of my presentation is about the politics of illness narratives.
Every illness or story has rules governing it: a politics. We all know that not all
illnesses and conditions are the same. That is obvious. Most people, however,
are not aware that the narrative one can tell about an illness or disability is
affected by certain parameters and that these parameters have real effects on the
story, the story-teller, and the people who listen to the story.

Again, I asked a series of questions. When I have asked them to North
American audiences, I get fairly uniform responses. It shows me that there are a
set of values and discourses about illness that are largely shared by audience
members. I expected to get more variation in this audience and I was right.
Some of the responses were counter-intuitive to me and required explanation by
the participant. These are the kinds of responses that stretch me the most, for

they speak to experiences I haven't had or customs with which I am not familiar.

I asked the audience, as I would ask the reader, to think of one effect of these conditions on the story, the story-teller or the audience to the story:

- *If the illness or condition is widely understood?*
- *If aetiology is known?*
- *If it is common?*
- *If there is treatment?*
- *If there is a cure?*
- *If there is no stigma attached?*
- *If it is inexpensive to treat or cure?*
- *If the illness itself produces no isolation?*
- *If the treatment of the illness requires no isolation?*
- *If there is no particular meaning attached to the illness or condition in one's ethnic group?*
- *If the incidence of the illness or condition is not related to factors of race, gender, class or ethnicity?*

Now imagine the opposite conditions:

- *If the illness or condition is* not *widely understood?*
- *If aetiology is* not *known?*
- *If it is* not *common?*
- *If there is* no *treatment?*
- *If there is a* no *cure?*
- *If there is* no *stigma attached?*
- *If it is* expensive *to treat or cure?*
- *If the illness produces* isolation*?*
- *If treatment requires* isolation*?*
- *If there is* special *meaning attached to the illness or condition in one's ethnic group?*
- *If the incidence of the illness or condition is* related *to factors of* race, gender, class or ethnicity*?*

Narrative analysis

In the workshop, I then presented my own and my daughter's illness narrative to illustrate the concepts I will describe below. Our illness narratives reflect our class position in North America. We both have medical insurance that pays for the best standard of care. This promotes a belief that if there is treatment, one should accept it and try for a cure.

The events in our story would unfold very differently if we could not afford or had no access to quality medical care. For instance, if after feeling my first breast lump, I knew that treatment existed but I also knew that I would be unable to get it, my illness narrative would have evolved very differently. The points I make about illness narratives make sense in a particular cultural context.

The beauty of doing a workshop among people from a variety of cultural backgrounds is that it is possible to draw on the range of experience in the room to place the theoretical points in cross-cultural perspective. For the purposes of this paper, I am abbreviating the personal story I told:

My partner, Hilary Worthen, and I became parents in the context of my mother's dying from a rare malignant tumor. Our first child, Ben, was born six weeks before my mother died.

Miranda was born two years and nine months after Ben. She was diagnosed with Beckwith-Wiedemann Syndrome at four hours of age by a paediatrician who had, by chance, delivered another baby with Beckwith-Wiedemann Syndrome exactly one year before. (Later, we were to learn that at that time, 1979, there were only eight known children with Beckwith-Wiedemann Syndrome in our region.)

Beckwith-Wiedemann Syndrome, or BWS, is caused by a mutation in chromosome 11 and most cases are thought to be sporadic as opposed to inherited. Infants with BWS usually have an enlarged tongue, abnormalities of the umbilicus, for instance omphalocele, and are atypically large. Many affected infants have hypoglycaemia at birth and it is speculated that this, if untreated, is responsible for the frequent occurrence of mental retardation. Children with BWS are at greater risk than the normal population of developing malignant tumours, of having enlarged internal organs, and of developing overgrowth of half of their limbs.

I was diagnosed with breast cancer in 1988, and then again in 1993. I have several relatives who have had breast cancer, and although their situations are not identical to mine, we can talk about shared aspects. While Miranda worries about the pervasiveness of breast cancer in her family, she is also aware that it produces a community of shared experience for me. This shared experience is missing for her because there is no-one in the extended family who shares her condition.

Miranda looks 'normal' but abnormal things happen to her, sometimes when she is just standing still. This can happen anywhere. Her joints dislocate easily. She often uses splints, braces or canes. She sometimes faints when she changes position from sitting to standing or lying down to sitting. As a young person, other children found this very odd and suspected her of faking. She has bad headaches that make her feel sick much of the time. Her inner organs don't function smoothly. She has many quirky ways of learning, although this has not prevented her from attending a selective university. Much of what happens to her body is uncommon. Even her learning difficulties are odd ones.

When her troubles began to accelerate during adolescence, we used externalisation to separate her from BWS. This was a critical distinction in our family. BWS takes up a huge amount of our family energy and resources, but Miranda often gets lost in that and doesn't get much attention at all. We try to keep BWS in its place so that it doesn't take over Miranda's life or ours.

By the time Miranda was 16 years old, externalisation was insufficient to protect her from feeling bad about herself. Contacts with doctors who didn't understand her troubles and didn't help, disappointments with friends who found her situation 'weird', discouraged her.

One day, I was preparing to work with some colleagues in New York, and Miranda dislocated her hip sitting on the couch watching a football game with her father. I had to leave while her father took her to the hospital and kept me posted while I was away for two days. When I came back, I was desperate to help her. I stayed up all night thinking about what we could do.

This analysis started that wakeful night. It focuses on a comparison between my illness narrative, a breast cancer narrative, and her illness narrative, which is a BWS narrative. It focuses on differences in our experience that derive directly from the kind of story we can each tell. Though much can be explained by virtue of the different roles that we play in the family, the differential resources these roles give us access to, and the nature of the conditions themselves, we have felt certain that other parameters are at play.

By virtue of having a rare genetic disorder that virtually no-one has ever heard of, Miranda is more isolated in her experience than I, who have a disease that affects one in eight women at some time in their life. At my age, it is hard to imagine that I might know or meet someone who does not know a woman who has had breast cancer. By contrast, it is hard to imagine that Miranda will ever find anyone who knows someone with her syndrome.

The disparity shows up in the health-care community as well. In the twenty years that we have been interacting with the medical profession over concerns related to Miranda's syndrome, and we have easily consulted with or met 100 doctors, only a handful have ever personally worked with a child with Beckwith-Wiedemann Syndrome. By contrast, all my medical providers have other patients with breast cancer.

The difference translates into very particular experiences that we each have on a daily basis. I never feel alone. I know that there are many women and many families who are going through what I have and my family has gone through, even right on my block! Miranda always feels alone.

Many people understand the aetiology, pathophysiology and the course of my illness. If I go to my public library, I can find reference books and first person narratives, even my own book[5] about living with breast cancer. No-one understands Beckwith-Wiedemann Syndrome. It is a disorder with multiple manifestations which can affect a number of organ systems and no-one can predict what is in store for any one person with the Syndrome. If Miranda goes to our public library, she will probably not be able to find even the name Beckwith-Wiedemann Syndrome in any of the 350,000 books in the library.

The name I use to define my medical situation - breast cancer - is defined as a disease and this fits with my experience of having had breast cancer. Each time I was diagnosed with breast cancer, the treatment that followed corresponded with my ideas of what having a disease entails. Though I had no pain from the lumps themselves, the surgery, chemotherapy, and radiation therapy I underwent confirmed my belief that I had a disease.

Miranda, on the other hand, carries a diagnosis that has no obvious implications. We know that she has BWS, but nothing inevitably follows from that diagnosis the way surgery, for example, follows from the diagnosis of breast cancer. When I told others I had breast cancer, most people could imagine what I was experiencing. When Miranda says she has Beckwith-Wiedemann Syndrome few people have any idea what that means for her.

Nor have we been able to find a word that conveys to us, much less to others, what she experiences routinely. Does she have a disease, an illness, a condition, a disability, a chronic disability, a chronic illness, a handicap, a disorder, a genetic disorder? We are baffled. No designation maps the territory. Without language, experience dissolves. Without language, experience cannot be shared and community cannot be formed.

Drawing on narrative theory, we now use three concepts routinely to make sense of our experience: narrative coherence, narrative closure, and narrative interdependence.[6] These narrative concepts are not neutral but are loaded with cultural specificity. There are class, ethnic, religious, perhaps even national biases embedded into this classification schema. The schema has been very effective in making sense of our illness experiences. It has been effective in helping Miranda feel empowered in her life, both with friends and medical personnel. The schema obviously fits with values and discourses that shape our lives.

Narrative concepts

Narrative coherence

Narrative coherence is established by the interrelationships between plot, character roles, and themes or values. In an illness narrative, the patient, the patient's family and medical personnel all play parts. With the diagnosis of breast cancer, a plot sequence unfolds according to fixed and known responses to data derived from the analysis of breast tissue. The patient will likely have visits with an oncologist, a radiotherapist, a surgeon and ongoing relationships with them depending on how the plot unfolds. Family members can be given a likely set of events to expect. The feelings of everyone involved are likely to include sadness, anxiety, worry and fear. This was so for me. Though, at any moment, I may have felt confused, the story I could tell was not particularly confusing. In fact, it was quite coherent.

By contrast, these elements applied within the context of Beckwith-Wiedemann Syndrome have the feeling of a deck of cards thrown into the wind. Having such scanty criteria available to us to guide our selection of cards - choices - it always feels just shy of random that we are proceeding, playing, with one hand of cards and not another. The significance of any event is unknown, thus the plot unfolds chaotically. Nor is it clear who the players - beside Miranda, Hilary and me, that is - should be. Do we go to a geneticist or a paediatrician? Do we find a specialist for each affected organ? How should we feel about it? Is this a disaster waiting to happen? Has a disaster already happened?

Narrative closure

The second feature of narrative that applies to illness narratives is that of narrative closure. One aspect of narrative closure is cultural resonance. The more familiar people are with the situation described, the higher the cultural resonance will be and the more likely that others will be able to participate with the person whose narrative it is in a way that supports, endorses and elaborates the story the person has to tell.

Breast cancer narratives have a high degree of cultural resonance. Within the last decade, there has been a very active breast cancer advocacy movement that has kept information about breast cancer highly visible to the public. It would be unthinkable today for a woman who has found a large breast lump have a friend or physician respond, 'Oh, gee, don't worry about that large lump'. One way of conceptualising why such a response is almost unimaginable today has to do with the high degree of cultural resonance breast cancer narratives have.

On the other extreme, Beckwith-Wiedemann Syndrome has low cultural resonance. Few people know how to respond when faced with the name of the disorder or even the names of the physical manifestations. Some people respond to their lack of knowledge with curiosity. Unfortunately, many more respond by withdrawing or operating from erroneous assumptions, wrongly generalising from other situations. This occurs with lay and medical personnel alike.

Narrative interdependence

Narrative interdependence refers to the interrelatedness of one person's narrative to another's. In families, one member's narrative is usually interrelated to the narratives told by other family members. For better or worse, my breast cancer narrative is related to the stories other women in my family with breast cancer can and do tell. Miranda has her own story that relates to my breast cancer because, as the daughter of a mother with breast cancer, she worries about her own increased risk of acquiring breast cancer.

Miranda's illness narrative has no connection to the illnesses of anyone else in our extended family. Though Beckwith-Wiedemann Syndrome is genetic, she is the first person in the family to be affected by it. This probably means that in her case BWS is a new mutation that appears for the first time in her. However, along another dimension, neither Miranda nor I could tell an authentic account of our lives without reference to the illness experience of the other. In this sense, our illness narratives are profoundly interdependent.

Applications

In our lives, we have used this analysis in a wide variety of ways. It helps us explain responses we get from friends, family members and health-care providers. It has been protective for us. It has also generated a number of specific coping strategies, several of which are described in a paper that Miranda and I published.[7]

In this workshop, I asked each person to work in small groups and to:
tell your own illness narrative or that of someone you know well. See whether these categories are useful to you in your story-telling. We have a wealth of stories in this room. See what we can learn together about the values and discourses that are embedded in these categories as ways of understanding illness. For instance, if you live in a culture in which scientific truth is not what is most highly valued, then are the effects of

telling an incoherent illness narrative different than if science is valued highly? Is a coherent illness narrative primarily important in a culture that places a high premium on scientific explanation?'

I circulated among many of the groups, listening as people applied this analysis (and another set of narrative concepts that I had described) to their own lives. After an hour, we returned to the larger group and people described what they had taken from the exercise.

It is not always easy for me to tell my own illness narrative and that of my daughter. Sometimes, it happens that a workshop or speaking engagement will coincide with a period in our lives when one or both of us is in significant distress. Telling our story takes on a poignancy that is almost unbearable.

The day I gave my presentation, I was in pain that was manageable. Hearing the stories in the small groups, talking with people in the large group about their experiences, participating in the proliferation of knowledges people have about themselves by providing language for the inarticulate body so that it too has voice, is the heart of meaning-making for me at this time in my life. It is doing what Miranda, aged sixteen years, asked of the family and friends she invited to a ceremony to witness the history of her living with BWS: it is 'nourishing hope and opposing despair'.

I am profoundly grateful to have had the opportunity to share this work with so many people from all over the planet at this conference.

Notes

1. Kathy can be reached at 82 Homer Street, Newton Centre, MA 02459, USA, email: kweing@aol.com

2. This conference was an exception. The Conference Collective had set up two booths outdoors attended by two masseuses who were available each of the three days for short or long massages.

3. Weingarten, V. 1977: *Intimations of Mortality*. New York: Knopf.

4. Weingarten, K. & Weingarten Worthen, M.E. 1997: 'A narrative analysis of the illness experience of a mother and daughter.' *Families, Systems & Health: The Journal of Collaborative Family Health Care*, 15(1):41-54.

5. Weingarten, K. 1994: *The Mother's Voice: Strengthening intimacy in families*. New York: Harcourt Brace.

6. Chatman, S. 1978: *Story and Discourse*. Ithaca: Cornell University Press.

7. See footnote 3 above.

Other references on illness and disability that readers might find of interest:

Altman, R. 1996: *Waking Up, Fighting Back: The politics of breast cancer*. Boston: Little, Brown.

Boss, P. 1991: 'Ambiguous loss.' In Walsh, F. & McGoldrick, M. (eds), *Living Beyond Loss: Death in the family*. New York: Norton.

Butler, S. & Rosenblum, B. 1991: *Cancer in Two Voices*. San Francisco: Spinsters Book Company.

Directory of National Genetic Voluntary Organizations and Related Resources, 1992: Chevy Chase, MD: Alliance of Genetic Support Groups.

Foucault, M. 1975: *The Birth of the Clinic: An archaeology of medical perception*. Trans. A. M. Sheridan Smith. New York: Vintage.

Frank, A.W. 1991: *At the Will of the Body: Reflections on illness*. Boston: Houghton Mifflin.

Frank, A.W. 1995: *The Wounded Storyteller: Body, illness, and ethics*. Chicago: University of Chicago Press.

Goffman, E. 1963: *Stigma: Notes on the management of spoiled identity*. New York: Simon and Shuster.

Grealey, L. 1994: *Autobiography of a Face*. New York: Houghton Mifflin.

Griffith, J. & Griffith, M.E. 1994: *The Body Speaks*. New York: Basic Books.

Hockenberry, J. 1995: *Moving Violations: War zones, wheelchairs, & declarations of independence*. New York: Hyperion.

Lorde, A. 1980: *The Cancer Journals*. San Francisco: Spinsters/*Aunt Lute*.

McDaniel, S.H., Hepworth, J. & Doherty, W.J. 1997: *The Shared Experience of Illness: Stories of patients, families, and their therapists*. New York: Basic Books.

Merker, H. 1992: *Listening: Ways of hearing in a silent world*. New York: Harper Perennial.

Panzarino, C. 1994: *The Me In The Mirror*. Seattle, Washington: Seal Press.

Register, C. 1989: *Living with Chronic Illness: Days of patience and passion*. New York: Bantam Books.

Rolland, J.S. 1994: *Families, Illness, and Disability*. New York: Basic Books.

Saxton, M. & Howe, F. (eds) 1987: *With Wings: An anthology of literature by and about women with disabilities*. New York: The Feminist Press.

Scarry, E. 1985: *The Body in Pain: The making and unmaking of the world*. Oxford: Oxford University Press.

Whitman, J. 1993: *Breast Cancer Journal: A century of petals*. Golden, CO: Fulcrum Publishing.

Williams, D. 1992: *Nobody Nowhere: The extraordinary autobiography of an autistic*. New York: Avon Books.

Williams, D. 1994: *Somebody Somewhere: Breaking free from the world of autism*. New York: Times Books.

Zola, I. 1983: *Missing Pieces*. Philadelphia, PA: Temple University Press.

3.

Developing relationships, performing identities

by

Gene Combs & Jill Freedman[1]

Since engaging with narrative ways of working, one of the aspects we have found most helpful is the idea that identity can be approached as a project. We make ourselves and each other up through the directions in life that we choose. Different possibilities for identity are opened through examining and revising relationships with problems and relationships with particular discourses and cultures. Equally significant possibilities are created by exploring ways of further developing thick and rich experiences of the relationships we have in our lives with other people.

When we think back on our workshop we remember the people who were there - the stories they told, the looks on their faces, how they made the room come alive. They joined with us in telling stories about and honouring the relationships in each of our lives that shape and sustain our preferred identities - our 'best selves'. Together we reflected on narrative practices, unpacking the many ways that they can bring forth new relational identities. We showed video-tapes of some of the people we work with talking about places and people who contributed to their identities, and we did an exercise to explore some of the ways narrative practices can be used in projects having to do with identity.

We put up the following lists on the overhead. We hope they give you a hint of some of the discussions we had, first about dominant discourses in our culture that stand in opposition to ideas of relational identity, and then about some of the narrative practices that build on and help develop the experience of relational identity.

Discourses that interfere with notions of relational identity

The following is a list of names that hint at different overlapping discourses, each of which is at odds with a relational experience of identity. It is not a complete list, and the names we use here may not be the ones that you would use. We would be curious to know what you experience as you read through the list. Are there important discourses that aren't mentioned here? If so, we would be interested in hearing your additions to the list.

* Separation/individuation
* 'Rugged individualism' (the loner-hero)
* Othering (dividing practices)
  Individual, pathology-based diagnosis
  Racism
  Classism
  Heterosexism
  Nationalism
* Self
  'Essential' or 'core' self
  Self-actualisation
  Self-esteem
  Self-reliance
  Self-policing
* Person as container (container metaphors)
  Inner strength
  Self-contained
  Resources (finding it within)
  Inner child
  Repression (of emotion, for example) and the need for expression

- Boundaries
  'Strong fences make good neighbours'
  Psychological discourses that privilege confidentiality, containment, and individuality over spreading the news, interdependence, and community

Narrative practices that presuppose the notion of relational identity

Some readers may not be familiar with all these practices; others may not see clearly how some practices presuppose and rely on the notion of relational identity. Nevertheless, we hope that reading over this list will give you some experience of how important relational notions of identity are to this work.

- Re-membering
- Documents (documenting new relationships with problems and projects)
- Letters
- Leagues/teams
- Outsider witness groups (reflecting teams)
- Accountability practices
- Situating
- Collaborating
- Externalising (changing relationships with problems)
- Inquiry into the effects of discourses (questioning relationships with discourses)
- 'Taking it back' practices
- De-centering

With these ideas in mind, we offered the following exercise as a way for people to explore some aspects of relational identity in their own lives, and, in so doing, perhaps to re-experience and thicken preferred aspects of their identities. We now offer this exercise to you. It is written to be done in pairs, but you could also guide yourself through it step by step.

Exercise: Relational identity

In pairs, ask your partner to identify:

- Someone from the past who she has always known was a significant person in her life.

- A group, ideology, or movement that she has felt very much a part of (for example, the anti-war movement, a church, or a sports team).

- A problem with which she has revised her relationship.

Then help your partner to develop three different sketches of herself as she knows herself through her relationships with the people or things identified above.

Start by asking your partner to tell the story of the relationship, and then ask questions that invite her to name her identities in the different relationships.

Sample questions for relationship 1:

- *Can you tell me a bit about your relationship with this person?*
- *What did this person most appreciate about you?*
- *If you saw yourself through this person's eyes, how would you describe yourself?*
- *What were you in touch with about yourself when you were with this person?*
- *What did your being this way (the way described in the answers to the above questions) contribute to this person's life?*
- *How would you describe your identity in this relationship?*

Sample questions for relationship 2:

- *Can you tell me about your participation in this group or movement?*
- *If you actively chose this group or movement, what about it attracted you?*
- *What were you affiliating with in joining this group or movement?*
- *What can you see in yourself in reviewing your participation?*
- *What did you contribute to this group or movement?*
- *If I could interview other members, what might they tell me about you? What was it like having a sense that others saw you in this way?*

- How [these could be very small ways] was this group or local version of the movement different for your having participated in it?
- Were there times in relation to this group or movement when you felt like you were participating in something larger than yourself? What was that like?
- How would you describe your identity in this relationship?

Sample questions for relationship 3:

- Can you tell me about this problem as you used to experience it? What were some of this problem's effects back then?
- What has changed about your relationship with this problem? How did that change come about? Were other people important in facilitating this change?
- Now that you have changed your relationship with the problem, what is different about your life and relationships?
- What do you know now about yourself that you didn't know when the problem was obscuring your view?
- How does your new relationship with this problem affect your contributions in the world?
- If the problem could speak, what would it most respect about you as a 'worthy adversary'?
- How did changing your relationship with the problem change your identity?
- How would you name or describe your identity in this new relationship with the problem?

Now, ask your partner to imagine, one at a time, seeing herself in each of these identities (or, if she already sees herself in this identity, ask her to see herself *more fully* in it). Here are some sample questions for this part:

- Is each of these different than your usual view? How?
- Do you like seeing yourself in each of these ways? Why?
- What difference would it make in your life and ongoing affiliations to keep each of these views alive?
- What difference would it make to the communities in which you participate if you more fully embodied these things in your day-to-day life?

Conclude this round by having a conversation about the process, the differences in the three views, and about whether there is a place (or could be a place) in your partner's life for all of them.

In conclusion, we'd like to say that this idea of relational identity has been a very enriching one for us, and one we've come to relatively late in life. That is, it is not part of the culture that either of us were raised in. We discovered at the conference that Aboriginal people have long had knowledge of relational identity. Our experiences in Italy lead us to believe that Italian people also value creating their identities through relationship. We feel fortunate to be able to share in some of these practices that for others have been ways of life for generations. We hope that the exercise enriches your experience of relational identity and inspires you to find new ways to make use of the experience in your life and work.

Note

1. Gene and Jill can be contacted at the Evanston Family Therapy Center, Evanston, Illinois 60201, USA, phone: (1-847) 866 7879, fax: (1-847) 328 1212.

4.

Buklod Ng Kababaihang Filipina

Filipino Women Survivors of

Family Violence[1]

Performing at the conference was a group from South Australia, Buklod Ng Kababaihang Filipina. *This is a group of Filipino women who have been meeting since 1993 when they participated in a series of cultural action workshops to address issues of violence. Through these workshops, they have developed a performance based on their own experiences. Most of the twelve Filipino women involved in* Buklod Ng Kababaihang Filipina *are survivors of abusive marriages to Australian nationals.*

A significant aim of their performances is to provide an acceptable and accessible medium with which to dialogue on violence against women in culturally sensitive and inclusive ways. Their performances increase the understandings and knowledge of Filipino experiences and present a unique and positive model of addressing the issues of family violence against Filipino women. What follows are excerpts from the script of their performance at the conference.

PART I: *For Better or For Worse ... Till Death Do Us Part?*

The Cast
Mother	*Juliet Espaldon*
Wife	*Sofia Albino*
Husband	*Nelma Roque*
Doctor/Husband	*Cecilia Remonde*
Mrs Brown	*Estella Salas*
Aleth	*Aleth Woo*

Synopsis of scenes
Scene 1: Tableau Group Ensemble
Scene 2: 'Where's the Door?'
Scene 3: 'The Jail Keeper'
Scene 4: Song: 'Oras Na'
Scene 5: 'I Want to Keep My Baby'
Scene 6: 'The Nursemaid'
Scene 7: Finale, Song: 'Ako Ay Babae' (I Am a Woman)

PART II: *Social Justice: Rights to be Safe and Free*

Synopsis of scenes

Scene 1: Poem: 'For the Skinhead Who Attacked Me in a Mall' (written by
          Ritchie Valencia-Buenaventura), recited by Nelma, Sofia and
          Cecilia.

Scene 2: Song: 'Time to Change' (Buklod version)

Scene 3: Song: 'Newsbreak' (Filipino Murders and Disappearances), presented
          by Nelma, Flores & Cecilia.

Scene 4: Finale, Song: 'Fight for Our Rights' (borrowed tune from 'Blowing in
          the Wind')

PART I
For Better or For Worse ... Till Death Do Us Part?

Scene 1: Tableau Group Ensemble

Scene 2: 'Where's the Door?'

(The mother wakes up late in the morning as the youngest daughter has been up all night. She is trying to prepare the children for school as well as mending a much-needed school uniform.)

(While the mother is mending, the father walks in.)

Father: Where's my coffee?

Mother: Coming dear.

Father: Where are my shoes? Have they been shined already?

Mother: Yes dear.

Father: Where's my breakfast? I told you to prepare everything in the morning on time! Do you expect me to work without having breakfast? Remember, you depend on me. If I don't go to work, you have nothing to eat.

Mother: Don't you know I have plenty of work in this house? Only this morning I didn't manage to prepare your breakfast on time because I woke up late. You know very well I didn't sleep the whole night because our daughter is sick. Can't you see all of you are demanding on me? You can't even help or make your own breakfast. I tried very hard to catch up with all the work on time but I can't. The five of you are depending on me. This is too much.

Father: Stop it. What do you think I am doing at work? Having a picnic?

Mother: And what do you think I'm doing in this house? Sitting pretty all day?

Father: Hey! I'm the boss in this house. You do what you're told. And if I want something, I want it to be done now! Not later, not in five minutes, not in ten minutes, but NOW! UNDERSTAND?

Mother: You're getting too much! I couldn't even have a rest even for a
             little bit. Four children to look after, do all the housework, and
             especially you, you're so bossy! I do everything in this house but
             for you ... it's still not enough.

Father: STOP COMPLAINING! Remember, I got you from your poor
             country. There ... you could hardly eat three meals a day, while
             here, you have plenty of food to eat. Here, you have a TV ... a
             microwave ... You don't have to wash clothes by hands and you
             don't have to gather wood for cooking. What are you still
             complaining for? So, shut up!

Mother: Don't tell me to shut up! I didn't marry you so that I can eat three
             meals a day. I even ate 4-5 times a day back home. I married you
             because I love you, understand? I got an education. I finished my
             college degree. I had a good job, a good life before you married me
             and you know that. (pause) Where are all your promises that you
             will give me a better life ...? Where's that loving, caring and gentle
             person that I married before? And where is all the respect that
             you've shown me before ...? All those are gone now. You don't
             even show me a little respect. You ignore me. You don't talk to me
             anymore, as if I don't exist. I only exist at mealtimes. You only talk
             to me when you want something. You didn't tell me that I'm your
             number six wife. You didn't tell me that I have to look after all
             your children from your previous marriages. So, what else do you
             want from me? I serve all of you. I do everything in this house.
             You don't need a wife, what you need is a housemaid.

Father: Alright! If you don't do what you are told to do, there's the door.
             Get out of my house.

Mother: Yes, I'm leaving you. Enough is enough!

Scene 3: 'The Jail Keeper'

Husband: Linda, from now on, you are my wife, listen to me. When I tell you
             to do something, you do it, do you understand?

Wife: Yes, Michael.

Husband: Can I have a cup of coffee?

Wife: Yes, Michael. Black coffee or white coffee?

Husband: White coffee with two teaspoons of sugar. Have you seen the newspaper?

Wife: No, I haven't seen the paper.

Husband: Have you finished the washing?

Wife: Not yet. Every morning after our breakfast I always mop the floor and do the gardening. And you ... you do nothing, always reading and watching the television.

Husband: Shut up! I'm going out to buy some food for the dog.

Wife: Michael, while you're out, can you buy me a lipstick and an eyebrow pencil? Please.

Husband: You don't need that rubbish stuff on your face.

Wife: Alright. Fine. Just don't forget to get some fish and rice on the way. I miss the Filipino food, you know.

Husband: Do you have some money for your food?

Wife: You're the one holding the money, you haven't given me any, not even one dollar.

Husband: (Goes to lock the door)

Wife: Why do you lock the door? I'm not a prisoner.

Husband: Oh, shut up, Linda.

Wife: (Watches him leave.) (Talks to herself) I am now nearly one year in Australia. Since I arrived here, my husband never let me eat my own Filipino food. He says it is shit food. I tried to be a good wife to him by following whatever he said. My husband does not let me go out of this house and the eight-foot fence around the house is like a prison. This is the time I miss my family back home the most, where I had freedom. (Pause) When he locks me up in the house all day, I think of my family and the food ... the *adobo* and the *bagoong*. I remember the happiness we all shared together during the Christmas celebrations. The whole family from my great-grandmother, great-grandfather, uncle, aunties, nephews, nieces, and the rest of the family gathered together to celebrate Christmas. I can see the happy faces, laughing, crying, hugging and singing.

(Sings the following song in her dialect - Dandansoy)

Dandansoy biyaan ko ikaw	*I'll be leaving you*
Pauli ako sa payaw	*I'll be going home to my cottage*
Ugaling kung ikaw idlawon	*Just in case you miss me*
Ang payaw imo lang lantawon	*Just gaze towards my cottage*

I miss the singing. He won't let me. I can't go to church. I haven't met other Filipino women. I'm not allowed to speak my language. He does not want me to meet other Australians; so I can't improve my English. I want to take English classes, but he won't let me.

Even when I'm tired, I still do the ironing. He would shout at me saying, 'You're a lazy woman', or sometimes, 'worthless woman'. My husband does nothing except reading the newspaper, drinking coffee and beer, and watching TV.

I can't live like this. I have to make a decision right now. I want to get out. I want to leave Michael. (As if speaking to Michael ...) I want to leave you, Michael. No, no ... he won't let me go. (Pause) (She decides to leave without telling him, before he gets back. Sighs ... gathers her sense of courage as she unties her apron, holds it in mid-air and looks at it.) That's it, Michael, I am leaving ... (Drops the apron on the floor). I have had enough. (Goes to leave the room, turns her back and has one last look, surveys the room, her life here, then turns and leaves.)

Scene 4: Song: 'Oras Na' (There's a Whisper)

May bulong, dinggin mo	*There's a whisper you listen*
Ihip ng ating panahon	*In the breeze, in the wind*
May sigaw, dinggin mo	*There's a cry, you listen*
At ubos na ang oras mo	*'cause your time has come*
Oras na magpasya	*It's your time to decide*
Kung saan ka pupunta	*Which way to proceed*
Oras na, oras na	*It's the time, it's the time*
Mag-iba ka ng landas	*To change your pathway*
Tayo na sa liwanag	*Let us follow the light*
Ang takot ay nasa isip lamang	*Fear is only in your mind*
Tama na ang pag-aalinlangan	*Let's stop having doubts*
Ang takot ay nasa isip lamang	*Fear is only in your mind*
Kung daa'ay di tiyak	*If you're not sure of the way*
At ang ulo'y laging ligaw	*And your heart is misleading you*
Damhin mo, damhin mo	*You should think, you should think*
Ang landas ng puso mo.	*Both dictates of heart and wind.*

Scene 5: 'I Want to Keep My Baby'

Aleth: Good morning Doctor.

Doctor: Good morning Mrs Kosti. How are you today?

Aleth: Not too bad Doctor.

Doctor: What's the problem? How can I help you?

Aleth: My period is late.

Doctor: Mrs Kosti, did you bring an early morning urine sample?

Aleth: Actually, I have Doctor.

Doctor: Okay, I will take it for a pregnancy test. Well, this will only take a few minutes. If the test is positive, a blue line will appear in the first window. How would you feel if you are pregnant?

Aleth: I want to have a baby but my husband does not want it.

            (Pause. They both look at the test.)

Doctor: Well Mrs Kosti, the test is positive. Assuming your last period was on … this would make you seven weeks pregnant. (Doctor notices Aleth feeling worried and confused.) Are you happy?

Aleth: I am happy and at the same time very worried. My husband doesn't want me to have another baby because he is too old. He wants to retire. Doctor, will you help me talk to my husband?

Doctor: Well, if you want to keep the baby, talk to your husband first, then we will make an appointment for you and your husband. We will talk about this matter further.

            (At home)

Husband: (Calling her) Aleth …! Dr Hocking rang me today and wanted to know what we have decided to do? I thought you already made an appointment to have an abortion. What happened in your last appointment with the doctor?

Aleth: According to the ultrasound result, I am twenty weeks pregnant. And it's a boy, Manuel.

Husband: What? You are twenty weeks pregnant? You are a liar. You knew from the beginning you were having a baby. I thought you were only two to three months pregnant. Boy or girl, I don't want any more children. One is enough. I will talk to the doctor and arrange something. Aleth, listen to me. I love you. But long before I told you I don't want children. Besides, I am embarassed to have small kids. Now, go to our doctor to have an abortion. I already arranged it.

Aleth: (Pleading) Manuel, I want to keep my baby. I want this baby. He will be a great help to us in the future. (Determined) I do not want an abortion! (Backing off)

Husband: Aleth, please understand me. If you do not want to destroy our marriage, take the baby away. (Pause ... trying to maintain his temper) You will destroy me. You will put me in jail. You can leave me. (Shouts) Now, get out of this house before I kill you. The door is open.

(Husband exits. Aleth walks downstage centre)

Aleth: I love my baby
My flesh and my blood
You have no right to destroy his life
As you will be taking my life away too.
I have a vision of my baby
A beautiful boy
Who will be my comfort and my joy.

I know he could grow up to be an upright man
Whom I can be proud of
And lean on
And be a good friend to his sister.

But he insisted to kill my baby
I cried for days not knowing what to do
I can't live with a guilty conscience

So, to the Lord, I called for help
This is my choice ...
I will keep my baby
My own flesh and my blood
You have no right to destroy his life
And mine, too.

(The ensemble comes downstage for finale.)

Scene 6 - The Nursemaid - Mrs Brown

Estella: First of all, Mr Brown and I were writing to each other as penpals.
After one year he went to the Philippines to see me. I met him at
the airport. When the plane arrived in the airport I heard someone
calling my name, 'Estella Salas, come inside the airport'. So, I
went inside the airport and I saw Mr Brown sitting down. I went to
him and said, 'Hello, I am Estella Salas', and he said, 'I am Jim
Brown'. After a few minutes I took him to his apartment. I visited
him every day at his apartment and we talked to see if I liked him
or he liked me. Then we arranged our marriage. After one month
we got married. The next month he came back to Australia and I
was left behind because my papers were not yet ready. Two months
later I followed him to Australia.

When I arrived in Australia, it was summer time and it was very
hot. I didn't know that Mr Brown was a very sick man. It was the
beginning of my worries. My problem in the summer was Mr Brown
couldn't breathe, so I helped him by rubbing his chest and back. And
in the winter time I helped him, too, by giving him massage. I
massaged his arms, knees and joints because of his arthritis. I took
care of him for eight years. Year after year. After eight years he got
very sick and I could not help him any more, so I called an
ambulance. After one month staying in the hospital, he died. I felt so
sad and lonely. In one year I was always crying. Nobody visited me
because I had no friends in the country. I was alone in the house. I
moved to the city so I could meet friends. Now I am living in the city
alone and I'm still lonely. This is the end of my story.

Scene 7 - Finale, Song: 'Ako Ay Babae' (I Am a Woman)

Ako, ako, ako ay isang babae	*We are, we are, we are women of the world*
(3x)	*(3x)*
Ako ay isang babae	*We are the women of the women of the world*
May baninindigan	*We do have conviction*
Sa kinabukasan	*In the near future*
May kalayaan	*We will have freedom*

PART II

Social Justice: Rights to be Safe and Free

Scene 1: Poem: 'For the Skinhead Who Attacked Me in a Mall'
Written by Ritchie Valencia-Buenaventura, Sydney
(used with kind permission)

Nelma: I should have run after you.
And hit you with my umbrella.
And called you names.
But because I grew up
Where the quiet and meek are preferred,
I was overcome by fear and shock,
And could do nothing else but weep.
And as I rode on the train I saw this written:
'ASIANS TAKE JOBS!
ASIANS GO HOME!'

In the land of my birth, the land that I left,
Which they say is a haven
for the violent and the evil,
a world of rebels of the left,
the right and the center,
a nest for kidnappers,
Hold-up men and snatchers,
not once, did this ever happen to me.

I am not a doll,
I am not a toy.
I am not a pet for you
to grab, fondle and kiss.

Cecilia: They say it was all my fault.
I shouldn't have walked down the road.
Certainly not in the Mall.
I shouldn't have been a Woman.
I shouldn't have been a Filipino.

They say it is not the worst.
Norma. Taunted and pushed by white
children at the train station.
Evelyn. Trembling as her panting doctor fondled her.
Linda. Teenagers in a car spitting at her.
My mother-in-law. Kicked by teenagers.
The daughter of Mr Santos. Beaten by white teenagers.

Sofia: This is not the worst.
Elsa. Married and a prisoner at home.
Lita. A prisoner at home, constantly beaten.
Teresita. Constantly beaten, she was murdered.
Annabelle. Strangled and her body cut up.
Rosalie. Strangled and burned.
Mila. Deaf-mute. Bashed in the head.

All: We are not dolls.
We are not toys.
We are not things
for you to spit on,
trample, and burn.

Nelma: We never intended
to snatch
the land that you stole.

Sofia: All we want are
some little corners
where we can live
in peace.

Cecilia: You have no right
           to rob us of
           honour and dignity
           just because you gave us permission
           to enter your paradise.

           We are not dolls,
           we are not toys,
           even migrants when oppressed
           seethe, rage, fight.

Scene 2: Song: 'Time to Change'

> *We must work now and live a brighter life*
> *We must not wait 'till it will be too late*
> *It's the time to change a violent world*
> *And care for all women*
> *And surely, we'll be there.*

> *We've been oppressed and exported by our land*
> *We give and give 'till nothing's left at hand*
> *It's the time to change a violent world*
> *And care for all women*
> *And surely, we'll be there.*

Scene 3: 'Newsbreak' (Filipino Murders and Disappearances)

Nelma: Good evening everyone ... This is a newsbreak.
         Australian men are marrying our women and killing them too ...
         and they're getting away with it. Is it because we are women ...
         and we are not white?

         In 1981, Teresita Andalis, 21 years old, was murdered for
         insurance. David Mathieson, her partner, insured her for four
         hundred thousand dollars in Australia and London, but failed to
         collect the money because he was found guilty of murder. The
         Brisbane criminal court sentenced David to life imprisonment.

Flores: In 1987, Rowena Sokol, 17 years old, of New South Wales, was shot five times. She died. Her ex-husband was found guilty of manslaughter and sentenced to 10 years jail. He was released after three years.

Cecilia: In 1988, Bella Elmore, 28 years old, of Western Australia, was pushed into the water. She drowned. Her sailor husband was jailed.

Nelma: In 1989, Mila Dark, 39 years old, of Victoria, was found dead ten kilometres from her house. Her husband was acquitted of the murder of his wife due to lack of evidence. Mr Dark went back to the Philippines and got another wife.

Flores: In 1987, Lusanta De Groot, 35 years old, of New South Wales, and her eleven-month-old baby were repeatedly hit on the head with a hammer. The baby died. Her husband Jacob subsequently committed suicide by jumping off a cliff.

Cecilia: In 1989, Generosa Bongcodin, 34 years old, of Victoria, died of strangulation. Her husband was found guilty. He was jailed.

Nelma: Also in 1989, Teresita and Normita married to the Garrett brothers, were found dead with their husbands. It was ruled as quartet suicide. One of the brothers/husbands had a severe illness.

Flores: In 1988, Jean Angela Keir, 22 years old, of New South Wales, was reported missing. Her husband was investigated for her disappearance. Meanwhile, Thomas Keir married another Filipino, Rosalina Keir.

Cecilia: Oh yes ... and Rosalina Keir, 24 years old, was found strangled with a lamp cord and set on fire. The police started investigating the possible link between the death of Rosalina and the disappearance of Jean. Thomas Keir was acquitted due to lack of evidence.

Nelma: In 1993, Elizabeth Mary Haynes, 5 years old, and Johanna Rodriguez, 12 years old, of New South Wales, were strangled and suffocated by their father. Mr Haynes was found guilty of manslaughter instead of murder. He is serving six years jail.

Flores: In 1993, Mila Wills, of Queensland, deaf and mute, was bashed on the head with a piece of wood. Her husband was found guilty and imprisoned.

Cecilia: In 1993, Elma Rebecca Young, 42 years old, of Queensland, was reported missing by her husband. Elma's body was found dumped by a roadside near her home. She was five months pregnant. Paul Young, 42, senior police constable, was her husband. Finally Paul was charged with manslaughter.

Nelma: Other unsolved cases reported were that of:

Nanette Villani: her decomposed body was found in Victoria in 1989. Eve Roweth was stabbed to death in 1991. Pia Navida's body was found in 1991. And Annabel Strezelacki of Claire, South Australia, was reported missing on 5th June 1998.

NEWSBREAK STATEMENT: Since 1980 to date, 4 children have died, 24 women have been murdered, 4 women and 1 child have disappeared. MAY THEIR SOULS REST IN PEACE ... (Repeat in Tagalog) ... SUMALANGIT NAWA ANG KANILANG MGA KALULUWA.

Scene 4 - Finale, Song: 'Fight for Our Rights'
(Sung to the tune of 'Blowing in the Wind')

How many deaths shall we see and count
Before our laws will be changed?
Yes! How many slaves must a man get
Before we can say he is banned?
The answer my friends:
There's not much being done
The answer: there's not much being done.

How many rapes must the women take
Before courts will work for our sake?
Yes! How many times can the men turn their heads?
Pretending they just do not see.

The answer my friends:
There's more to be done
The answer: there's more to be done.

How many times do they want us to cry
Before we will have their reply?
Yes! How many deaths will it take till they know
That too many women have died?
The answer my friends:
We fight for our rights
The answer: let's fight for our rights.

How many children must plead to be free
Before men will let them just be?
Yes! How many children shall be sacrificed?
Before justice is realised?
The answer my friends:
We fight for our rights.
The answer: let's fight for our rights! (2x)

Acknowledgments

Special thanks for support and assistance go to:

The Department of the Arts and Cultural heritage, SA; Dawn House SA Inc (formerly Women's Emergency Shelter, North Adelaide), SA; The Aboriginal and Multicultural Women's Project, SA; The Lutheran Community Care, Blair Athol, SA; Enfield Uniting Church, SA; The Philippines-Australia Solidarity Group, Victoria; Enfield A Together Against Crime, SA; Centre for Philippines Concerns, Brisbane and Melbourne; Richie Buena Ventura, NSW; David Wilson for Photography, SA; Graham F. Smith Peace Trust Fund, SA; Babette's Eatery, Semaphore, SA; Blue Expressions, Custom Art Framing, Semaphore, SA; Henley-On-Sea Café, SA; Imprints Bookshop, SA; Limbos Haircutters, SA; Dheera Payler and Visarjan Barker, SA; Sisters-By-The-Sea, Semaphore - Sister Bookshop of Murphy Sisters, SA; Domestic Violence Unit, SA; Riverland Women's Emergency Shelter, SA; Murray Mallee Community Health Centre, SA; Adelaide Women's Community Health Centre, SA; FACS Reference Group on Cultural Diversity and Quality Development Unit, SA; Women's Shelter Housing Association, SA; Kilburn Community Legal Services, SA; Reclaim The Night Committee, SA; Women's International Day Committee, SA; Multicultural Domestic Violence Action

Group, SA; Women's Health Statewide, SA; Women's Emergency Services Network (WESNET), Canberra City; Dulwich Centre, SA.

Note

1. The Filipino Women Survivors of Family Violence can be contacted c/- Dawn House, PO Box 47, Campbelltown 5074, South Australia, ph: (61-8) 8365 5033. Chairperson: *Sofia Albino*; Secretary: *Aleth Woo*: Treasurer: *Nelma Roque*; Advisors: *Joan Dicka* (c/- Dawn House), and *Suzanne Elliot* (community development worker, Inbarendi Wadu Project [Coming Together in Communication and Partnership], 85 Hookings Tce, Woodville Gdns 5012, South Australia); Director: *Tarnya Van Driel* (c/- 5/323 The Esplanade, Henley Bch 5022, South Australia, phone [61-8] 8353 5454).

Day Two

5.

Conference news
Extracts from the newsheet that was distributed on the second morning

Each day of the conference we produced a small newsheet to act as a forum of communication between the collective and the participants and between participants themselves. We used this forum to ask for feedback on various issues and to clarify practical arrangements. Throughout the conference various participants announced in the newsheet a variety of informal events including an Indigenous People's meeting, a discussion about young people and drugs, a Jewish gathering, and an opportunity for lesbians to get together over lunch. We also used the newsheet to invite participants into considerations of care-taking. Here is an extract from the conference newsheet that was distributed on the second morning.

Taking care

On all three days of the conference there are a number of sessions and keynote addresses in which people are telling their stories of survival.

A lot of care and effort has been taken to create a good context for the people who tell these stories. The lead-up to the public telling of these stories has occurred over many months. There's been a lot of thoughtfulness in relation to ensuring that the presenters only tell what is right for them to tell. Many of them wrote their stories as a way of taking care and being certain about what they wanted to say.

We also thought a great deal about what would be appropriate for the speakers in relation to the way participants responded to them. In most cases we decided against the sessions being open for questions.

Some presenters have chosen to have a rehearsal of their talk to groups at Dulwich Centre and often this was followed by a group acting as a reflecting team. Some of the presenters in the conference have decided to have a reflecting team after they speak rather than taking questions.

The plenary speakers were all given a choice as to how they wished to meet up with people after they had spoken. These informal catch-ups under trees will be facilitated, but in the end the presenters retain the right to speak only about what they wish to.

A sense of connectedness has begun to develop between those who are sharing personal stories as they have attended each other's rehearsals. Over these three days these connections are sure to strengthen.

A context of care for participants

The days of the conference are very long! We'd really like to again invite participants to skip some sessions and just relax. It's going to be sunnier today and tomorrow so people can go and sit down by the river and reflect.

We're conscious that new awarenesses may come from witnessing the personal presentations, both for members of dominant and non-dominant groups. If people need to talk anything through in relation to this, please approach us and we will try to create a good context for the conversation.

If anyone is thinking of setting up a small group discussion around a particular topic and would like to talk through ways of going about this, come and speak with us. Today with the better weather these conversations could occur down by the river.

It seems important to acknowledge that as participants in the conference we bring a great diversity of histories to these three days. The stories that are told in presentations will resonate differently between us - both the stories of injustice and the stories of survival. How can we, as participants in the conference, keep an awareness of this with us? How can we best draw upon the resources of our diversity to act respectfully and take care of one another throughout the witnessing of powerful stories? If people have further ideas about this we'd love to hear from them - both in terms of this conference, but also in terms of possible future events. Perhaps people could write down their ideas and place them in our suggestion box - in the Publications room. Thanks.

6.

Redefining a version of family and nationality

by

Leonie Simmons Thomas[1]

For a long time, my story of where I have come from, and where I am, has been fragmented. The different aspects of my experience seemed too complex and segregated to be summarised in their entirety. However, as I slowly took each piece of my life and listened to what it had to say, I soon discovered that my story drew itself together. It now seems more complete than I had ever given it credit for.

Although there are many experiences of youth which most people can identify with, every individual holds a unique story of what it is like to be a young person.

For me, the joys and sorrows of adolescence were accompanied by the consequences of being an Australian girl with a Vietnamese heritage. I was adopted as a young baby from Saigon into an Australian Anglo-Saxon family and therefore my difference from my peers and the majority of my community has been outstandingly obvious. My diversity has not hindered me from happily and positively living my life – but it has always been there, sitting in the periphery and waiting to be addressed. It was during my teenage years that I had a feeling of displacement in regards to where it was that I belonged. I was

56

born in Vietnam yet I was unable to identify with an Asian culture, and I was raised in Australia yet I was not entirely characteristic of that nationality either.

Initially, I attempted to ignore my Asian origins and spent my early teenage years trying as hard as I could to dissociate myself from my mirror image. However, I lived in a predominantly Anglo-Saxon society and I could not avoid the subtle reminders that I was different to the accepted norm. Fitting in is a pretty healthy desire, but when you always have a sneaking suspicion that you don't fit in, it can cause the kind of pain that is silent and constant. Throughout my years at high school I was embarrassed by my physical appearance, and somehow being different was internally translated to being ugly and invalidated.

After I left school, and during my university studies, I began to accept that I needed to come to terms with who I was and not what I thought I should be. I realised that in wanting to 'fit in' I had ignored the instances where I had always felt uncomfortably excluded. There are many experiences of my youth which can still occur today which act as reminders of my diversity.

Within the first instance of meeting people, perfect strangers will assume that it is okay to ask personal questions as to where my parents come from. And it is not uncommon for people to make uninformed references to 'my' people, 'my' language, and 'my' country. It would upset me that I felt the need to justify my residency. Although in my heart Australia was my one and only home, the fact that other people assumed that it *really* wasn't hurt very deeply.

The experiences that come from being a Vietnamese-born Australian living in a white society are not that much different now from when I was in my teen years, except now I do not feel the same embarrassment, confusion and anguish. I have since learnt and continue to learn to distinguish the difference between a person being genuinely interested in my life and an insensitive interrogation by people who need to feel comfortable with who lives in this country and why.

I no longer accept that I have dual identities but acknowledge an oriental ancestry and an Australian citizenship as being a complete category of my own. I now celebrate the peace that I have made with my identity and the lack of justification that I give to it.

As well as having to create my own definition of nationality, I have also needed to reassess the meaning of family. In general I have found that the accepted concept of family is defined and validated by biological commonalities. However, my experience of family has not had anything to do with blood relationships.

Although I have a mother, a father, and three brothers, I have no known family medical history, no family tree, and no family resemblances. For many people it is difficult to understand how it is that I consider my family to honestly be my family, and that I could accept and belong to people whose biological genes I do not share.

In the past, if somebody has perceived my relationship with my parents as being close or not close, it has been attributed to the fact that I was adopted. I cherish my family, we fight and we have our fair share of problems, but this is all in spite of the fact that I first came to my parents at an airport and not at a hospital.

I am often told that it is such a shame that I do not know my 'real' family, as if my adoption is a pretend situation for when my real life comes along. It is true that my mother did not give birth to me, but both of my parents have given me life, as well as a sense of family that I have inherited which does not deserve to be undermined. For me, family is about the connection which comes out of shared experiences, temper tantrums, laughter and growth and, if blood is thicker than water, then unconditional love is stronger than genetics.

My personal story has revealed to me that adversity does not necessarily have to lead to delinquency, and difference does not have to result in dysfunction - and therefore my interest in youth issues is grounded in discovering with young people the best possibilities which can be realised when the worst expectations are not fulfilled.

Note

1. Leonie can be contacted c/- Dulwich Centre Publications, Hutt St PO Box 7192, Adelaide 5000, South Australia.

7.

Amy Ralf's[1] story

In 1995 I wrote a story. It was Amy's story and it told of my life as the daughter of a lesbian and how this affected my experiences of education. Since that time, the response I have received from those who read my article has helped give me the strength to change my story. For a lot of my life I felt that my lifestyle was too different to talk about. I felt vulnerable around most other young people and was convinced that my sort of lifestyle did not exist outside my family and most definitely not at my primary school! Since the publication of my article, in which I was identified only by my first name, I have received some inspiring feedback, in particular that from other young people. This feedback told me that what I had written had helped then fight feelings of 'abnormality' and this has been very powerful for me. This to me shows the importance for young people to have peers from a diverse range of backgrounds. This, in my opinion, can help them to be themselves and to value who they are.

When I wrote my story, it was only as Amy. At that point I would not have been able to identify myself without the fear of recognition. This fear stemmed from a belief that recognition of my situation would ultimately lead to rejection. But today, I am here not only as Amy, but as Amy Ralfs, because now I can reveal who I am without that fear. In fact I was even able to invite my school principal to hear me speak today! My ability to do this is partly due to my recognition that my mother's lesbianism is only one of the many differences which help to make my life unique. The more I recognise the positive influences that these differences have on me the more I am able to do away with many of my feelings of isolation and 'abnormality' which came from keeping such a big part of my life secret.

There are many people and aspects of my life which differ from the norm. My family is not merely those whom I am related to by blood, nor is it restricted to mother, father and siblings. I have many women in my life who have been signed up as 'aunties'; I have cousins who have been more like sisters; I have my mother's partner of ten years who has been like a parent to me in that time; I have an uncle who has been like a father (and is the most qualified unemployed person I have ever met!) and I can count people from various backgrounds among family and friends. While I find I have gained from living with and around so many different people, there seems an inability by others to accept them as my family. On my thirteenth birthday, when I introduced three women as aunts, my friends needed to sit down and try to work out the biological connections, rather than accept that they were people I considered family. I believe that it is necessary for the definition of family to be broadened and the conventional labels, which are all too readily employed, removed. In the eyes of present day society I would be viewed as the only child from a single parent family. However, to describe myself as this is to make invisible many of the people who play a part in my life. It has been this experience which has taught me to look for the stories behind the imposed labels. At one point these labels greatly affected my experience of the world outside my family, but now I have been able to see through their power. The restrictions inflicted by these classifications leave no room for your story to be heard, and this silencing can be very damaging.

The diverse array of people within my life has allowed me to challenge the concept of normality, which plagues so many young people in particular. In the face of what is portrayed as 'normal' in regards to family or lifestyle, it is often easy for young people to feel isolated and marginalised because they perceive themselves and their experiences to be 'abnormal'. From this position many come to disregard the invaluable learning that these experiences can provide. In my life, it is the incredible uniqueness of all of my family and friends and their acceptance of each other that allows me to be the individual that I am. The wide range of opinions gives me the opportunity to challenge and be challenged as well as discuss issues, and the many different life experiences help me to increase my understanding of the world.

However, whilst I have become much more at ease with my life and the people in it, I still at times find it necessary to explain myself to others.

Recently, I was in this situation and had to tell a friend of my mother's lesbianism. It was not that previously I had been hiding it but that it feels so normal to me that I forgot that it was something that was necessary to spell out in so many words. Her response when I told her was to me a very telling remark. She said: 'I thought so, but it's not exactly something you ask is it?' and she was right. Society is so geared towards heterosexuality being the accepted lifestyle that again this concept of 'normality' restricts us to blatantly accepting that that's what everyone will be. So far none of my friends have taken me aside to whisper in my ear: 'Amy - my mum's heterosexual'. Maybe if society wasn't so quick to label you as being one thing or another, it would not be necessary for whispering of this kind to take place. I believe that the more we can come to identify and value the positive influences that the different aspects of our lives have on us the more genuinely we can know each other. The sooner we are able to stop using labels to classify people, the sooner we will be allowing ourselves the opportunity to enrich our own existences with a greater understanding of the stories of others. By living with the differences that exist in my life, I get a taste of the extent of diversity in the world. I am grateful for this opportunity because it means I know the value of listening to the marginalised voices of society.

Note

1. Amy can be contacted c/- Dulwich Centre Publications, Hutt St PO Box 7192, Adelaide 5000, South Australia.

8.

Does the future echo positive movement?

by

Roxanne Adams[1]

Hello. I'm the state co-ordinator and a spokesperson for Future Echoes - an organisation run for and by young people who have lived in care. We're called Future Echoes because we don't want our future to be an echo of our past or present. Things ... people ... can always grow or change for the better.

I have an absolute commitment and passion to young people in care. That commitment comes from my own history of being in care. I have two older sisters, one younger brother and a very special Mum. Unfortunately for our family, my Mum developed schizophrenia in her mid-twenties. As a family, we lived with Mum's slow deterioration for about twelve years. Sometimes we would have to live in a women's refuge or go into short-term foster care or group homes when Mum was having a difficult time of it, but we managed to stay fairly well together until I was nine.

When I was nine, Mum had to be institutionalised and us kids were put under the Guardianship of the Minister - Minister Dad.

Being in care has shaped and impacted upon my life in a great variety of ways, but nothing changed my life or my family like the day it was decided that my Mum would never recover, only deteriorate, and that her children would never live with her again.

Today, many years later, my mother and I have been reunited. I have, after hurdling many barriers, become my mother's legal guardian. She now lives in the same state as me and is once again someone I love to be with and someone who chills me right out. Even though she doesn't speak, we communicate really well - in particular, I can tell when she's annoyed with me! Anyway, it's great to have a grounding in life again, and for her, I know it's great to once again have a role in her kids' lives. No-one in welfare respected or understood the full ability and capacity of this relationship, although I was supported by Marion FAYS[2] to go to the Tribunal hearing. So ... I'm back to hanging out with my Mum like before I went into care - very cool ...

But what was it like to be in care? No two people ever have exactly the same experience of the state care system, so I must say, whatever I describe my experiences to have been, they are mine only. I cannot talk for others. It is hard to know how to describe being in care, because to describe it is to describe a whole lifestyle, a large part of my identity and an array of incidents, emotions and relationships. In one heaped, sad and sorry bundle of words, I would say being in care is like this:

it is the pain of abuse
the frustration of bureaucratic inefficiency and neglect
the loneliness of separation
constant disappointment
the feeling of not belonging
broken trust
the insecurity/instability of multiple placements
the necessity to simply survive rather than live
constant feelings of responsibility and guilt
long hours waiting in government agencies

As I have attended conferences on child abuse and neglect, I have witnessed a whole variety of discussions on all sorts of horrible abuses - emotional, sexual and physical. I have been surprised, however, that no-one discusses what all children and young people in state care face - systems abuse.

What is systems abuse? It is the bureaucratic inefficiency and neglect I spoke of earlier. It is when the system forgets it is dealing with human life which lives longer than 9 till 5 Monday to Friday. It is when second best will have to do in light of government funding cuts. It is when myself or my family are shifted from placement to placement, suburb to suburb, school to school, because they could not find a permanent placement, or because the home was closing down, or because it was policy that people couldn't stay at that place for more than three months, or because no-one wanted to take four children, or because we weren't the right age for the picking - all of these things were out of my control and in the hands of the system.

Systems abuse is that I can't escape the responsibility that has been assumed and forced onto me for my little brother. It's that I have attempted suicide because I can't escape that. I've always had people - foster mum, social workers - say to let him go. Yet when the going gets tough, welfare dumps him on my door. What's that about? All the words of what to do and what not to do, dissolve into reality when there's a lost soul in front of you.

Systems abuse is a portion of adults unable to make simple decisions. Even if we wanted a bit of practice at it, the decision has to be made quickly, or it's confidential, or you're too young, or it might bring stuff up, or you're not interested anyway ...

Systems abuse is also the inappropriate placement of children, which more often than not leads to devastating results. Systems abuse is also feeling invisible. I never felt anybody was really looking out for me, me individually, before things go wrong, not just after.

Systems abuse is that some workers feel so overwhelmed that they see sending a birthday card to the young people they are supposed to be working with as yet another thing to do, rather than as a small piece of joy to share, or as the least a child can ask for.

Systems abuse is not preparing young people for life after care or independence. There is no aftercare for wards of the state. Unlike other young people who often have someone to look out for them after they turn 18, for state wards it's often an abrupt transition. Preparation for leaving care and the teaching of life skills is without a doubt an area of youth welfare that needs urgent attention. Of all state wards:

- 75% will leave school with no qualifications
- 50% will be unemployed
- many will become homeless - 50% of homeless 14 to 17 year-olds have a care background
- and some will go to prison - 25% of the adult prison population has a care background.

These statistics are people's lives. Generally speaking, kids go into care because of abuse. They've already been abused; they don't need to get systems abuse on top of that. We have to find ways of providing better care for kids whose families have fallen apart.

On the other side of the coin, being in care was also inspiring, fulfilling, powerful and educational. These positive aspects arose from the negative. In the face of adversity, some people become better or stronger. I am one of those people. Had I not been in care, I would not have many of the qualities that make me who I am today. I would have to say that, despite any hardships I may have encountered by being in care, I know it has shaped my life in a more positive way than remaining home would have.

Had I not been in care, I would not have met the great multitude of people that I have - and the silent learning that goes with that has made an immense impact on me. The observation of living with people for too short a time to bother conversing has meant I really understand what it means to have an objective view - and I'm not being negative, this really is a great gift. I can deal with change, which is something life will always throw - but some don't take well. Importantly, I have met people who really care. I have been able to challenge people - including young people - to care, and I have had the time and experiences to analyse what this care/love thing is anyway. For some of my foster parents, this has been really important, and quite a struggle, and I feel I have been given early warnings and other people's learning on this stuff. It makes a big difference when you think about the fact that young people from a disadvantaged background are taken advantage of so much.

Having lived in care also meant I was introduced to Future Echoes. All of a sudden there was this useful channel for the whole mess I just spoke of. All of a sudden I could DO something with the knowledge of my experiences, rather than dwell on them. Through my participation I've been able to see that it was all worth it - I can now help the child welfare sector to grow and move on. I feel very useful and that's how other kids at Future Echoes feel. All of a sudden we realise we're not just foster kids or whatever. We learn every day, we share our thoughts for others to build on, we try new things and fail together, and we're confident to tell others what we think because we've learnt no-one knows but us - we're experts.

So when I am asked what motivates me to work with Future Echoes, it is true that my past is a factor, but my brother's future, and the future of other young people in care, is even more motivating. Twenty thousand Australian kids in care are growing up fast in an unsuitable system.

So what would be a good start to improving the system?

I strongly believe that young people, workers and carers must have a more unified and co-operative approach. These three groups of people all say they want to achieve the same things for young people - that is, a happy and safe environment in which to live. Some of us young people may not be the brightest sparks in our age group but we do know what we like and what we don't like! We do know what services work for us, what workers we respond to best and why. These things are our expertise and these are the only things we need to know in order to improve child welfare.

I'm not saying that whatever a young person says or suggests should be adopted without discussion, compromise or change. I'm suggesting the method of 'ask, listen, then work from there'. If young people's ability to creatively problem-solve was more respected and encouraged, I believe we would see some great innovation in child welfare, not to mention young people with greater confidence and self-esteem, workers with more options and less resistance.

I believe some professionals see consumer participation as a difficulty because they feel as if they might lose control of young people. This is a fairly natural reaction for adults (in my youthful opinion) but I think this needs to be overcome as it is not about who has more say or control, it is about having a good working relationship and providing the best care possible.

At Future Echoes we come together as young people who have been in care. We organise training for young people so they may fully participate in the systems change that we make for all kids in care. We present at conferences, we give kids in care the opportunity to tell us like it is, and we contribute to the training of workers. Whilst we are primarily volunteers, we practise what we preach: we work hard to learn and use professional conduct in all that we do. For example, we take care not to break confidentiality through run-of-the-mill, obvious case studies or conversations in the corridor. And, professionally, we use fun, technology and our imagination as much as we can.

We also produce a newsletter that we attempt to get to all kids in care in South Australia. When you're growing up, you don't often realise that there are lots of other kids in care. Often, you're the only person in your school in care. It can be a very lonely sort of an experience. Being a part of Future Echoes is just the opposite. Finding out knowledge you have, meeting a new intelligent person inside you is like making a new friend and turning a corner. It's very welcoming to know that people understand that you can contribute, and are willing to support you in doing so.

Finally, I want to say that young people do respect and appreciate the tremendous work that is done for them. Young people may not be as vocal with their praise as with their complaints, but as an advocate for young people I do know that the majority are thankful to those who do their best to support them.

I look forward to seeing the powerful and positive change that comes from recognising not only the need to always move forward but also *everyone's* ability to participate in this - experienced, reality-based adults; desiring, creative young people.

Thank you.

Notes

1. Roxanne can be contacted c/- Future Echoes: phone (61-8) 8212 8055, fax (61-8) 8212 8055, email: FutureEchoes@bigpond.com, or write c/- 28 Peel St, Adelaide 5000, South Australia.

2. FAYS is an acronym for Family and Youth Services - a South Australian government department.

9.

Beyond the straight and narrow

by
Michael Miers [1]

*Michael Miers works with B-Friend and The Second Story (a youth
health service) assisting young people to 'come-out' and to come to
terms with issues of sexuality. He also gives guest speeches to teachers
and students in high schools about homophobia, sexuality and the
experiences of being a gay person.*

Hi. I'm involved in two different but related areas of work. I am a part of B-
Friend, an organisation which assists young gay, lesbian, bisexual people in
coming out. And I also work as a peer educator at The Second Story (a youth
health centre). I go into schools and speak about my experiences as a young gay
man.

So many things need to change in this society, sometimes it's scary, but
today I wish to focus on homophobia in schools.

In order to address homophobia, it's crucial that it is addressed in the
education system. Schools are a foundation of our society and culture. So much
of what we learn there upholds both justice and injustice. It can create a vicious
cycle. If we can just make some changes in schools, then maybe we could set
up a different cycle, a different loop, of beneficial change.

Most schools are not safe places for non-heterosexual people. Kids can be downright destructive about issues of sexuality. If you're not heterosexual and people know about it, chances are you're going to get continually harassed and bullied. And often teachers don't, can't or won't see or are not able to help effectively.

Currently the world is missing out on some of the potential of its youth. We have to find ways of taking the stress off non-heterosexual kids in schools in order to realise some of this potential. We have to find ways in which young people have more freedom to learn those things that are relevant to them with regards to their sexuality.

When I was at school we were shown only one form of sexuality - straight. Non-heterosexual lifestyles were maybe mentioned once. They were spoken about for two minutes, maybe less. Not talking about all the variations of human sexuality allows room for misinformation. It allows homophobia a greater foothold in schools and in society.

I reached a point in school where I became asexual. It was probably one of the most destructive states into which I entered. It ate at me. I had always been taught that being gay was wrong, so I began to hide my sexuality, not only from others, but from myself. I couldn't see any other alternatives. This caused a state of depression in which I considered taking my own life. Somehow, though, I just had to find a way beyond the straight and narrow.

A doorway

The first piece of information I came across was through a magazine. It was a glimpse of a doorway into another world. In this magazine, there was an advertisement about gay people. There was a picture of a group of guys and a caption that read 'Which one of us is gay?' Beneath the picture was a form you could cut off and send away for more information. I did this, and the information that came back was about the actual people who were in the advertisement - how old they were, their life experiences, the ways they came out, and their sexuality. It was a real eye-opener. While I was reading their words, for the first time, I realised I was not alone. It was a great feeling of affirmation.

The advertisement was put together by the Victorian AIDS Council. It was like they threw me a life-line. It had a major impact on my life. It was like the key to a door, but more than that it was like they were showing me the way! I took the key, I opened the door and found myself on a pathway that led to The Second Story - the centre for which I do some work these days. There I met other gay people around my own age. It was very confronting but it was a good experience. Meeting other guys made a big difference.

These were my life-lines, and in hindsight a cause of great relief. They are what I am now trying to offer others. When I was at school, if someone had come in and spoken of the existence of other ways of living, other than being heterosexual, I probably would have been much happier. I would have been able to come to terms with my sexuality a lot earlier. It would have shown me that it was all right, that I was okay.

If the young man I once was, the guy who was hiding his sexuality even from himself, looked at me now standing here in front of all of you, I think he'd be in shock. I don't think it would have been in his imagination that this could ever happen. He'd be amazed that I'm now in the business of building life-lines for other non-heterosexual students.

Celebration

As a part of my work with The Second Story, it's been great to go out there and show people that there's much to celebrate. It's validating for me. Taking action in trying to remove homophobia from schools gives me hope. Talking about my experiences in schools is an attempt to show the kids who might be non-heterosexual that 'it's okay'.

By being 'out', we show the broader community that it's okay to be gay! We are trying to destroy stereotypes that surround non-heterosexual people. By challenging homophobia and heterocentrism, we're endeavouring to educate the heterosexual community that non-heterosexuals are an integral and important part of today's society.

In schools everyone is led to believe that you have to 'fit in' and that you have to conform to fit in. What I'm saying is that you don't have to conform. There are other ways of living that go against the 'norm', whilst still being a part of society. It's important that young kids in schools realise that they're not alone and that difference is okay.

Off the straight and narrow

Finally, I would like to take this opportunity to dispel the myth that says your school years are the best years of your life. That is often not the case for non-heterosexual people. I have related to you, through personal experience, that it isn't easy being a non-heterosexual person in our schools and society.

Through my work with B-Friend and at The Second Story, I hope to make it easier for other people like myself coming through the school system. It is important that the message, 'homophobia is *not* okay', is developed and taught in schools. As part of this message, sex education programs need to be modified to include all aspects of human sexuality.

Despite all the negativities I have experienced and got through, I can assure you that life gets better when you're off the straight and narrow.

Thank you.

Note

1. Michael can be contacted c/- 10 Byrnes St, Brooklyn Pk 5032, South Australia, email: avatar@merlin.net.au

10.

The anti-harassment team: A presentation of hope

by
Esther Gatward, Anton Bruell
& Leilani Salesa[1]

The Anti-Harassment Team is a team of young people, within Selwyn College (Auckland, New Zealand), who respond to and act to prevent incidences of harassment and violence in their school. On the second morning of the conference, Anton, Esther and Leilani gave a plenary presentation in which they related stories to illustrate the possibilities for the transformation of school cultures when schools are willing to devolve power and when students have the opportunity and support to develop their own creative, vibrant and effective responses to harassment and violence.

Welcome by Esther

Tihei wini wini, Tihei wana wana, Tihei wa mauri ora.

Ko te mea tuatahi ki te atua. He mihi nui kia koe.
Ko ia ra he whakapono me te tumanako o tenei ao hurihuri.
No reira, he mihi nui ki te atua.

Ki nga tini mate, o tenei rohe, o tena rohe, kua wheturangitia.
Haere, haere.
Haere ki te timatatanga, me te whakaotinga o nga mea katoa.
No reira, haere atu ra.

Ki te whare nei, e tu, e tu.
Ko koe te taonga I whakapua wai tia nga ahuatanga o nga rangatahi o tenei ao. Ki te iwi nei I raro I te tuanui o tenei whare.

E kui ma, koro ma, tena koutou.
Nga kaiako, nga tauira, tena koutou.
Kia mau tatou te matauranga me nga tikanga o to tatou tupuna mo ake tonu atu. No reira, ko tenei te wa o whakaputa.

Tena koutou, Tena koutou, Kia ora te whanau e huihui mai tatou katoa.

Kia ora,

As a young Maori woman I come from a long tradition of *whai korero*, discussion as a means of coming to understanding and agreement. To the Maori, valuing the spoken word over the written has always been a vital part of our culture. A gathering of people to discuss affairs that have arisen within the tribal community, the *hui*, has meant that through the generations communication as a means of problem-solving has become a culture within a culture. Discussion has become just as important as any action. When you're young, however, taking action can be the easier option. For me, being part of the Anti-Harassment Team has meant an opportunity to present an alternative to young people.

Each member on the team brings with them their own definitions of conflict and understanding, built from a wealth of personal and cultural experience. I think it is this variety and difference that allows us to be flexible and creative in the way that we work as individual mediators and as a team. For me, the key to effective communication is for the person to be able to relate what is being said to their own lives. It is this personal link that has allowed the work of the Anti-Harassment Team to be effective as a culture in itself and to further the already diverse and progressive atmosphere of Selwyn College. Once an alternative way of thinking, an effective means of communication, has affected one person, it opens the way for it to become a way of life for many.

Kia ora.

Anton

We come from Selwyn College, a diverse school of many peoples - a significant number of them have only recently immigrated to New Zealand. Within the school we essentially have a cross-section of the whole world, about 56 different cultures. It's hard to imagine the life that some of our peers have led. The diversity of the cultures within Selwyn are represented here today by Leilani, a young Samoan woman, by Esther, a young Maori woman, and by myself, a young Jewish man. Different cultures offer different perspectives, so the diversity within Selwyn can bring with it conflicts, both old and new. But it also brings the potential for creativity. Within each cultural tradition are histories of addressing conflict and finding ways of living respectfully with others. The Anti-Harassment Team is a group of young people from a wide range of cultures who come together, train, and support each other to act as effective mediators. We are a team that enables young people who may not feel comfortable talking with adults about what they are experiencing, to turn to us. The team has developed into a partnership between the counsellors, Aileen Cheshire and Dorothea Lewis, and the team members. Along with the team back in New Zealand, there are many people who have enabled us to do this work and to stand here today. In my mind are the people who support us, particularly the staff who have encouraged this sort of work, and the young people who consult with us. For me personally, also in my mind are my family - my brother, who was on the team before me, and my family, my parents, who encourage me with the values they hold and the support they give.

Leilani

Talofa lava mo le ava noa. I would like to share with you an event that is precious to me and to the history of my people.

Tapua Tamasese was a Samoan paramount chief in the early nineteenth century. At the time, Samoa was governed by New Zealand. Amongst the people there was a great feeling of injustice - the people felt the government was failing to hear the concerns voiced by the people.

Tamasese led the Mau, a pacifist movement of civil disobedience opposing the New Zealand government, along the waterfront of Apia.

Tamasese led the people with peaceful intentions. He had empowered them to unite, encouraging them to stand together, as one.

The people were prepared to stand for their beliefs. However, they were not prepared for the New Zealand snipers who opened fire on the crowd, killing ten supporters and mortally wounding Tamasese. On his deathbed Tamasese urged that, though blood had been shed, the people must continue to act together in opposition to the New Zealand Government.

Tamasese's passion for his people, his commitment to justice, and his ability to empower others, is what motivates me, giving me strength, power and passion, enabling me to do what I do.

My *Aiga*, my family, give me strength and give me patience, which enable me to continue with the work I enjoy. The atmosphere and environment in which I was raised, with love, values and support, encourages me, gives me energy and determination to challenge situations and to work towards change. To begin with, I plainly accepted this work in knowing that it made a difference in the school environment, but, when we started to be acknowledged, appreciated, and respected beyond the school community, I realised the potential this work has to spread further and wider. I'm already part of something by being a member of the team, but for me to come here and to share the wealth of knowledge that belongs to the team is to realise the potential and take it even further. The learning involved in this work has been invaluable, enhancing the skills I already have and also offering me a new perspective. It's an awesome feeling to have the ability to make an impact and bring about change.

An interview with two faces of Harassment

We would like to introduce to you, now, the reason why our team exists. We would like to introduce to you two faces of Harassment who have very kindly agreed to be publicly interviewed, just this once.

Interviewer: Thank you for coming here today. Would you be able to tell us a little bit about where you come from?

Harasser # 1: Well, I've been around since the dawning of time.

Harasser #2: Yes, well, I'm everywhere: families, community, institutions, workplaces, especially in schools.

Interviewer: So, if you've been around such a long time, you must be pretty successful. How do you account for your success?

#*1*   Well, I work on people's ignorance.

#*2*   Thrive on competition.

#*1*   We do really well where people care about being different. Schools are my playgrounds.

#*2*   Yeah. The teachers really help us - they label people as victims and bullies ...

#*1*   ... and imply that the person is the problem. When people are labelled as victims and bullies and talked to individually, I can go right on in. That makes a perfect climate for me to get on with my dirty work and, well, people end up feeling as if it's them who's got the problem.

Interviewer: So, how about Selwyn College - have you been around Selwyn for a long time?

#1   Yeah, of course I have! Since the first day it opened.

#2   Just like any school.

Interviewer: What are your hopes for that school, what are your aims and ambitions?

#1   To make people's lives miserable - turn people against each other.

#2   To gain power by having people use me in dominating others and putting others down.

#1   Yeah. To be the main way that people relate to each other.

Interviewer: So how do you do that, how do you work?

#2   Well, we draw people into our way of working.

#1   Mmm, and become a habit. I've worked through generations and families so I become taken-for-granted and people don't see me any more.

#2   I make myself satisfying and enjoyable!

#1   Hmm. We become part of the accepted culture of how people relate to each other.

#2   Yeah. It comes back to the teachers, though. The best way has got to be through the teachers. They use their stand-over tactics in the classroom over the kids and then the kids find their anger and use it on each other in the playground. It's great! They must make it hell for each other to learn.

Interviewer: So you seem pretty confident and you work well by yourselves, but who are your friends?

#1   Well, Gossip and Lies ...

#2   Lies and Deceit ...

#1   Yeah, and Resentment ...

#2   Don't forget Jealousy ...

#1   Greed, and Deceit ...

Interviewer: What great company you keep! So, can anything stand in your way, you know, who are your enemies?

#2   We really don't have any ...

#1   Well ... there is something ... I guess when I'm exposed and when I'm named.

#2   Yeah, I suppose that's true, when people see through my tactics and start realising the effect that I've had on their lives, that can be a problem.

#1   Yeah, when people start to figure out my strategies and tactics ...

Interviewer: So, how can people do that, how can people spot you?

#1   Well, I'm pretty tricky and I've got all sorts of disguises. I used to show myself in obvious bullying and threats of violence, but one of my favourite tricks these days is when a group can be made to shut someone out by giving them the silent treatment.

#2   Yeah. We look for any way, any difference as a way of starting - sexuality, race, appearance - you name it, it's a way to get started.

Interviewer: So, right now, how great is your hold on Selwyn College?

#2   Right now? Gee ...

Interviewer: Do I detect that there might be some problems for you there ...?

#1   I've had a few difficulties at that school, because, well, the teachers there have these ideas, you know, about relating to students respectfully! And we had to work round this through other ways, through the students, because the staff had this weird idea about co-operating together! I mean, that made everything really quite difficult. And then, a few years ago, they started this dreadful thing called the Anti-Harassment Team.

#2   Yeah, but at the beginning, you know, we didn't think it would be too much of a problem. They only had, what was it, about 20 kids and a couple of counsellors and …

#1   Yeah, and we all know how easy it is to sneak around counsellors!

Interviewer: So, what is it about this Anti-Harassment Team that's so bad for you?

#1   Well …

#2   Well, I just can't get in there!

#1   Yeah, … they stick up posters and tell people about me, and, people aren't even afraid to talk about me any more. It's really bad! The worst thing is mediation, yeah, they have this thing they call mediation and it's shocking!

Interviewer: So, this mediation sounds pretty bad. What happens in a mediation, how come you walk away?

#1   Well, we just can't get it happening in there you know. It doesn't help that the school thinks they're really important and lets students out of class to participate in them …

#2   The teachers even respect them, mmm. [said with disgust!]

Interviewer: Can't you get in there at the very beginning?

#1   Well they do this thing called 'the introduction' and, oh gosh, we've got to sit out these things called 'guidelines' …

#2   Yeah … they have these agreements - that's a real problem. Well, from my point of view it can screw things up from then on!

Interviewer: So, what else is in these guidelines, these agreements?

#1   Well, the mediators, they explain that they're not there to solve the problem, but they're just there to get people working together, and then the people hear stuff directly instead of talking behind each other's backs.

Interviewer: So the mediators don't tell people off for doing your work?

#2   Oh no, they don't even give their opinion or anything. They just facilitate the direct talking. That's their job. And the trouble is, people don't get angry about being blamed, and they often start listening to the other person!

Interviewer: So what actually happens to you in a mediation?

#1   Well, at the beginning, the people get to talk about the effects that we have on their lives, which isn't actually all that bad. I mean, we get to sit in there and hear all about how much of it succeeded and all of our nasty tactics and how well they're working. That's pretty cool!

#2   Hmm, but the trouble is, when the people are working through it they often realise that it's not what they want for their lives and then they decide to get rid of me!

#1   Yeah, and what's more, Fairness often gets in there, and that's one of our biggest enemies.

#2   Yeah, then I don't stand a chance. The worst thing is that people come to agreements about how to stop me, and how to work together against me!

Interviewer: How do they do that?

#1   Well, part of it is through the agreements they reach, but the worst part is the direct talking, you know, that they then take into other situations. It makes Gossip not work around the school any more. And then they take it outside the school. Some of them even take it into their family!

#2   It's like a virus that spreads and infects groups of people! It's horrible.

Interviewer: But we've all heard about how strong you are, I mean, surely, you've got some ideas of how to work behind the scenes to get around this?

#1   Oh but these mediators, you know, they really know their stuff. They're incorruptible! And they can spot us a mile away!

Interviewer: How do they do that, can you tell us about that?

#2   Well here's an example. We were having a ball last year with these two groups of junior boys, 13 and 14 year-olds. There were about fourteen of them. It was a big group thing and everyone was at each other's throat. We had the best tactics going, you know, the teasing, the bullying, the knocking things off people's desks, stealing things, put-downs. It was looking really promising! We were really hot for these boys because they were making each other's lives a misery! We had big dreams for them.

#1   But then, one of them got fed up and organised a mediation ...

Interviewer: But surely a single mediator wouldn't have been much a match for fourteen boys and the two of you?

#1   Well that's what we thought, you know - fourteen boys and us, not a problem! But then not only did one mediator sit down with them, but two sat down in the room and they sorted out the whole thing. It was a sad, sad day ...

Interviewer: It seems like you sound worried - can you say a bit about that?

#2   Yeah, well, we're trying to think our way around it. I'm sure it's just a temporary setback. We've still got a bit of a hold in the school and we keep our hopes alive on the new juniors that come in each year.

#1   Yeah, they've got so used to me at primary school that I'll be able to sneak in with them into high school! I can also sneak in with the older new students, especially those that've been to single-sex schools - man, they are the best material!

Interviewer: So you sneak in there? But it doesn't sound like you manage to last very long ...

#1   Well, I'll give you another example. Recently, there was this girl I had got completely believing in me while she was at another school - it was fantastic! When she first came to Selwyn, she thought the only way to get people to like her was to be really tough and staunch. She carried the bullying atmosphere with her wherever she went and together we had developed it into a fine art. When she got to Selwyn she began to use all the usual tactics, but she got a real surprise when some other students told her she needed to go to 'anger management'! Then, when she got into an argument with somebody, they told her that the way to sort it out was to go to a 'mediation'. They wouldn't even let her have a fight! But I did manage to sneak into that mediation.

Interviewer: What happened?

#1   Well, the mediation had just began when she pulled a knife! I was really proud of her! The trouble was, the mediator just stopped the mediation.

Interviewer: Just stopped?

#1   I mean, she was really cool about it and everything, but she simply stated that the school had a policy of non-violence. The school backed her up on this and suspended the girl.

Interviewer: But surely suspension just breeds Resentment, and I thought Resentment would be on your long list of friends?

#1   Well, that can be true. If there's just a suspension, Resentment can have a field day. But in this school they use mediations after a suspension, and that's a real problem! I really thought I had this girl totally believing in me, but when she came back to school after the suspension she had a mediation. What a problem! She heard for the first time about the effects I can have on people, and she started to wonder whether my tactics were the best way of making friends after all. What's worse is that the others in the mediation heard that she was really lonely and said that they wanted to make friends. They told her that they would like to be friends and all she needed to do was make a new start without me! Well, that was it for me. I gave it up!

Interviewer: It sounds like you want to give up on the whole school ...

#1   Well ...
#2   No, not at all! We're sticking around. We've still got a good chance.
#1   But it is unbelievable how hard it's getting ...
#2   Yeah, but if we leave it here then we'll never be able to come back ...
#1   It's hopeless here, we've got to put our energy elsewhere!
#2   But this thing's like a virus, if we don't stop it here ...
#1   Look, do what you like, but I'm moving on ...

#2   What?! Are you going to wimp out on me again?!!
[They argue with each other, and then one walks out.]

Gossip and Rumour

As referred to by Harassment during the interview above, we have
recently begun to focus on the roles of some of Harassment's friends, especially
Gossip and Rumour. At the beginning of 1998, the team was experiencing
many mediations to do with the influence and effects of Gossip and Rumour
amongst 13 and 14 year-olds. The idea of inviting these students to externalise
and expose Gossip and Rumour was born. We hope the effects, tactics and
intentions of Gossip and Rumour will become clear, and that people will join
together to stand up to these powerful problems.

Of course, we can't really tell exactly what the effects of these
workshops have been. Many of them have been great fun, and certainly people
speak differently about Gossip and Rumour now - there is a language with
which to speak about them. When team members come into a classroom, get
everyone on their feet, give them roles, and begin role-plays, it is so enjoyable
and very different from adults coming in and telling people not to pass on
Rumours or Gossip.

Concluding story from Anton

To end, I'd like to refer to a story of mediation which I did about a year
ago. It was the story of Thulie, who is a young black South African woman, and
John, who was, for a time, a skinhead.[2] It was certainly one of the most intense
mediations I've ever been in.

It is our job, as mediators, to be even-handed, to contribute to an
atmosphere where people can talk to each other differently. When mediations
work well, we don't interfere a lot in the process. We simply ask questions which
open space for changes to occur.

Thulie's challenge to racial harassment was not just for herself: it was a
challenge on behalf of her people, and in a way for all people who live to see an

end to racism - including my people, Jewish people. As a result of the mediation, Thulie experienced a sense of pride which made it seem as though a weight had been lifted from her shoulders.

Looking back now, I realise that John reflected a lot on his views and ideals. He recognised the consequences of his behaviour, and realised that, at the time prior to the mediation, he was being a person he did not want to be. He started work on a new reputation.

My role as a mediator in the Anti-Harassment Team, and as the mediator in this particular mediation, was to make the process work, to remain even-handed, to mediate.

Farewell

Toi te kupu, toi te whenua, toi te mana.
Knowledge is the word, knowledge is the land, and knowledge is dignity.
Kia ora.

Notes

1. Esther, Anton & Leilani can be contacted c/- the Anti-Harassment Team, Selwyn College Counselling Dept, Kohimarama Rd, Kohimarama, Auckland 5, New Zealand, phone (64-9) 512 9610, fax (64-9) 521 9620.

2. For a more detailed explanation of this mediation, see 'Taking the hassle out of school and stories from younger people', *Dulwich Centre Journal*, 1998, Nos.2&3.

11.

Bringing spirituality into professional contexts

by

William D. Lax [1]

Spirituality can be a central aspect of many people's lives. However, it is often not made visible or acknowledged by professionals in their clinical work. Attention to spirituality is usually relegated to more 'specialised' therapists such as pastoral counsellors and ministers. This marginalisation is somewhat paradoxical and confusing, as religion and spirituality are often central and organising discourses in most of civilisation.

As narrative therapists, we have become very competent at identifying cultural narratives, particularly those that foster and support oppressive practices. We are able to facilitate our clients in identifying discourses (and practices) such as capitalism, patriarchy, homophobia, and racism and the roles they play in the development and support of problems in their lives. However, we have not been so adept in identifying cultural discourses that are supportive of individuals' narratives of liberation and preferred ways of being. While at times support can be found in discourses such as feminism and the 'counterculture', often these liberating stories are situated within more local contexts.

This workshop addressed how we might bring spirituality and religious practices more to the forefront of our work and how we might consider these to be a source of great support for developing and maintaining preferred ways of being for both consumers and therapists. Specifically, the workshop discussed how some ideas about Buddhist thinking and practices, as well as a wide range of other religious and spiritual practices, relate to narrative therapy and might be brought forth in our work. Participants were invited to talk about their own relationships to religion and spirituality, how they have been able to maintain these connections, and how these have influenced their thinking and work.

Throughout the workshop, participants acknowledged the importance of situating their comments within their own experiences and cultural backgrounds. The workshop allowed for multiple perspectives to be examined and addressed, including hearing from those who had both strong positive and negative experiences regarding spiritual or religious practices.

Initially, there was a presentation of some common theoretical assumptions and practices between narrative therapy and Buddhism. Assumptions included some of the following:

- Absence of 'truth'.
- Focus on personal experience.
- Language is not representational.
- Privileging the person's lived experience.
- Shift away from dualities.
- Stories are constitutive of world.
- Life is impermanent/always changing.
- Self arises in conjunction with others.
- Focus on political.
- Importance of community.
- Maintaining a non-expert position.
- Role of reflexivity; goal of liberation.

In discussing practices, comparisons were made between Buddhism and narrative along the lines of ideas about 'Problems, Persons, and Change'.[2]

- Problems are *effects* of desires or aversions and are external to the person.
- The idea of self is an illusion or a construction, as there is not a bounded, masterful self, but one culturally and contextually constructed.

- Change is the development of a position of non-attachment with attention to one's alternative, preferred identities within a community of others, filled with compassion and loving kindness.

The presentation part of the workshop concluded with a discussion of how I am influenced by Buddhism, what I pay attention to, and what guides my interactions with clients. These included the following:

- Attention to the role of the therapist as having a certain understanding about a path or model, but not confusing that with a position of authority.

- Value of concentration as necessary for mindfulness - it helps generate a sense of focus to facilitate a more detailed process of externalising, deconstruction and re-authoring.

- Labelling or externalising practices help recognise the object of attention more clearly, offering greater focus and precision in the conversation.

- Practice is changing our relationship to problems; it does not necessarily mean getting rid of problems.

- Not developing alternative, preferred ways of being that people then also become unquestioningly attached to.

- Notice and support relationships and narratives of generosity, loving kindness, compassion, equanimity, and acceptance.

- Value of support and communities of concern.

The second part of the workshop was spent in group discussions. The groups were self-selected, with people identifying and organising themselves along several different secular and religious/spiritual topics and areas. Participants were given the questions listed below and were asked to discuss these among themselves.[3]

Exercise/Questions

1. Identify a spiritual or religious practice or tradition that has been an important influence in your life. What are some of its values or assumptions that are still important to you at this time? Why are these important to you?

2. Are there some ways that you include these values and assumptions in your therapy practice, directly or indirectly? Specifically, how are these present in your practice?

3. If you were to incorporate these values and assumptions more into your therapy practice, how might you do that and what might be some of the effects on you?

The groups reconvened together after about forty-five minutes of discussion.[4] Conversation was centred on several areas, with most people reporting that they had a very personal experience in addressing the questions. Very few reported the same experience, although many said that it had helped them bring together their personal religious/spiritual traditions with narrative work.

After the workshop, numerous people approached me during the next few days. Again, they said they had very personal experiences that they will carry with them for some time. I was very touched by these comments and was surprised by the profound effects the workshop had on participants. The comments supported that idea that there is a strong need for these kinds of discussions to continue, with further exercises developed to help people examine their experiences around spiritual practices. It supported the position that greater efforts should be made to help move spirituality from the edges to the centre, a place where it exists in many cultures around the world.

Notes

1. Bill can be contacted c/- Antioch New England Graduate School, 40 Avon St, Keene, New Hampshire 03431, USA, phone (1-603) 357 3122, email: blax@antiochne.edu

2. My appreciation to Jeff Zimmerman for developing this format for discussion and presentation.

3. My thanks to Kiwi Tamasese for reviewing the questions before the workshop and offering her comments and revisions.

4. The Buddhism group did not return, as they became very engrossed in their conversation. They did tell me later that they had a wonderful discussion and planned on developing further conversations via email.

12.

Addressing troubles in therapy networks:

Towards collective responses

from

Dulwich Centre Publications[1]

This short article has been generated from a workshop that took place at the conference which tried to grapple with the question of how to address troubles in therapy networks. Since preparing for this workshop, we at Dulwich Centre Publications have ourselves lived through a complex and difficult situation in which at times troubles grew very large. It is with a sense of relief and hopefulness that we look towards expanding the conversation on these issues.

These conversations require the greatest of care. When trying to talk about troubles in our own networks we are stepping into areas of life that have often been associated with significant sorrow and heartbreak. Every utterance could hold different meanings and memories for different people.

From the responses we have received so far, both at the conference and since then, it appears that there are many of us who are asking the questions - How can we play a part in collective healing in our own networks? How can we develop community healing responses to conflicts/traumas in therapy networks?[2]

In the workshop, we tried to be very clear that we don't believe we have any particular expertise in this area, nor clear ideas as to answers to these questions. We do, however, have an almost overwhelming sense of waste in relation to all the anguish that we have witnessed within therapeutic networks over years, and a determination to find good ways of talking about possible healing community responses. It seems sad that so much of the energy of therapists goes into witnessing and responding to other people's troubles, and yet therapy networks are often at a complete loss as to what to do when trouble comes amongst or between our own.

In time, we hope that conversations will be generated around this topic that will offer practical tools in relation to understanding past experiences of troubles, assisting in addressing present issues, and/or preparing for the future situations that are sure to continue to occur.

How can we play a part in healing in our networks?

In our conversations, both in the workshop and since then, it has been really clear that many people are actively seeking ways of playing a part in collective responses to troubles. People spoke of wanting to respond in ways that were not in any way participating in gossip, while alternatively they did not wish to remain passive and quiet while trouble was having effects in their network. Here are some of the questions we have been trying to think through in relation to community responses.

- How can we develop community healing responses to conflicts/traumas in therapy networks - particularly networks in which people are working day-in, day-out with stories of conflict and trauma? When individuals are in conflict or trauma, what gets in the way of community responses? How can we overcome these restraints? Would it be helpful to create some sort of guidelines for the future - both within workplaces and within professional and personal networks?

- In trying to develop community responses, how can we take care to always take into consideration relations of power (gender, class, sexuality, race, age, organisational)?

- How can we be clear about the difference between standing above the troubles (taking either a 'position of judgment' or a stance of 'neutrality') and playing an *active* part as a member of the community to diminish acts of degradation and to find healing ways? (Would it help if we explored the distinctions between a commitment to 'neutrality' and a commitment to not participate in further dividing or degrading practices?)

- If we find ourselves 'in the middle' of other people's conflict, how can we speak for ourselves and not about or for others?

Exploring the difference between individual support and collective responses

When troubles do make an appearance in our networks often there is no lack of willingness on people's part to help. It is more a matter of trying to find what would be helpful and trying to avoid ways of escalating the conflict. One of the most interesting areas we have been exploring is the difference between individual support and collective responses.

- When responding to a 'trouble' between people, what is the difference between offering individual support, and playing a part in creating a collective response? What are the effects of these different responses? When are either/both appropriate? What sort of support might individuals need in order to participate in collective processes?

- How can we acknowledge the enormous amount of individual support that is usually offered during 'troubles', while at the same time be open to thinking through the limitations of individual support in some circumstances? How can we take care that by individually supporting one person, or even both people at different times, that we are contributing to a moving forwards rather than a solidifying of different realities? Are there more creative ways than just hearing out everybody's individual experiences? What would they be?

- What does the experience of witnessing one person's personal pain/trauma/ distress contribute to how people respond to the 'other' in the situation? How can we find ways of talking about the complexities these situations raise?

Towards collective responses

Within a culture that so thrives on individualistic ways of thinking and being, it can be challenging in times of crisis to try to act more collectively. In trying to think through what other options may be - community meetings, letters - we quickly became aware of what care is needed in these situations. So much of western culture's responses to troubles are grounded in philosophies of punishment and shaming, and community responses would in no way be immune from these tendencies. At the same time, searching out alternative philosophies and histories of collective responses could have much to offer. Here are some questions we may consider along the way.

- How can we find ways in which everyone who wants to contribute to healing can come together, acknowledge that the community is being affected, and talk through the roles that everybody can play in bringing about a just and fair resolution? What would make this possible? What sorts of acts of care would need to take place?

- If the people directly involved in the conflict or trauma cannot be involved in a collective healing, who can ensure that it happens? How can we take care not to burden the people directly involved, or diminish their experience of what may be profoundly painful times, while at the same time interrupt damage that is being done to broader relationships of which the people directly involved may not even be aware?

- When people have greatly varying understandings of the same events, or when far from meeting collectively, it would be better for the people at the centre of the troubles to go their separate ways, what role can the broader community play in ensuring that his process is as respectful as possible?

Language

Within the workshop there were also conversations about the use of language in times of conflict.

- While not denying the very real trauma that any of us can and do feel, how can we take care with the language that we use in times of conflict or trauma? How can we take care to ensure that if we use language developed out of political struggle (such as 'abuse of power', 'exclusion', 'silencing', 'marginalisation', 'powerlessness') that the ways in which we do so are not diminishing of the life-and-death struggles from which this language was created?

Structures of care for workers

Finally, we spoke about the responsibilities that we felt as members of the broader community to those therapists and others who work in areas of significant trauma.

- If people are working in areas of significant trauma, day-in, day-out, what structures of care are in place for these workers? Who takes care of these workers? What are our collective responsibilities to the people doing this work? How can we ensure that adequate structures are in place so that if a conflict or trauma does occur that it does not swamp these workers, does not, in some way, tap into all the other stories that they are witness to in their everyday working lives?

- In all our conversations, how can we take care to remain aware that many people who choose to work in the area of responding to abuse and violence, do so for very personal and heartfelt reasons? What difference would it make if we kept hold of this awareness at all times?

- How can we ensure that any conflict or trauma does not get in the way of, or diminish shared commitments? How can we draw upon and build upon collective hopes, intents, dreams, and faith at times of conflict?

A song of sadness and strength

We ended the workshop at the conference by singing a song. Here are its lyrics:

Sadness and strength

there are notes of sadness in this song
and notes of strength as well
we've gathered here
in careful conversation
with respect
and to move towards
healing

when every day we witness stories of grief
how can we ensure
that division does not infiltrate our networks
which we simply can't afford?

how can we use the skills we've found,
to help create
ways of collectively responding
to our own networks' heartache?
when every day we witness stories that sparkle
from them what could we learn?
are there helpful histories of our own networks lying silently?
how could they be uncurled?

there are notes of sadness in this song
and notes of strength as well
we've gathered here
in careful conversation
with respect
and to move towards
healing

Building a collective process

At the end of the workshop we invited participants to discuss and document the sorts of questions that they were interested in thinking about in more detail. As facilitators we collected these questions, and said that we'd publish a collection of them down the track. The only problem was, in the hustle and bustle of the conference, we think we lost some of the participants' written ideas! We are very sorry about this. If you have other ideas on this topic, and/or if you'd like to be part of ongoing conversations on this topic, please send your ideas and contact details to us here at the Publications as we hope to publish further on these issues at a later date. We would like very much to build a collective process to generate ideas and conversations on this topic.

Notes

1. The workshop in the conference was facilitated by Maggie Carey, Cheryl White, Shona Russell & David Denborough.

2. In this context the word 'community' could refer to a network of professionals; or to a 'community of care' that forms around somebody, or some people, at a time of crisis; or it could refer to a 'community of concern' - for example, people who all share a commitment to working in a particular area. In this write-up the word 'community' is used to mean all these things interchangeably.

13.

Introducing Mosaic

by
Penni Moss & Paul Butterworth[1]

Mosaic is an ongoing project run by young people around the issue of substance use. At the conference, an alternative resource was launched (also entitled *Mosaic*), which we hope will help to generate discussion across generations on the issue of drug use. We've included some extracts from *Mosaic* in this article.

Dear Reader,

Both of us are closely linked to social networks in which drug use plays a large part. Drugs are something many people enjoy and will continue to use, but we have also had to deal with the devastating effects that they can have on people's lives.

We wanted to find ways of addressing some of the problems without denying valid parts of our own culture. We thought there might be ways to create thinking around drug use which are less pathologising and more honouring of young people's experience and choices.

In this project we've tried to have a finger in both pies, to help create a working link between services and young users. The process of research has been both fascinating and informative. In Adelaide and in Sydney we visited youth services, health services, psychiatric institutions, drop-in centres, needle exchanges and the police. We spoke with other young people, and did a lot of background reading. We also attended the 1ˢᵗ International Conference on Young People and Drugs which was held in Melbourne.

What we learned has changed our own thinking and attitudes quite considerably. This work has given us the framework to challenge dominant ideas around drug use both in our own minds and in conversation with others.

We hope this resource will bring you as much insight as working on it has brought to us.

Part One: The Politics of Drug Use

In the broader culture, drug use is seen in many ways. It is seen as a medical issue, a psychological issue, an issue of criminality, a social issue. What is missing here is that drug use is primarily and embarrassingly a political issue.

Which drugs are legal and which drugs are illegal, which drugs are considered to be fine, and which ones are considered to be used only if you're really screwed up, is completely political. Locating the issue of drugs in the realm of politics is important. So many of the health consequences and the more problematic parts of drug culture are made drastically worse by the illegality of certain drugs and the sanctioning of others.

What difference would it make if everyone who drank alcohol or smoked cigarettes could have a glimpse of the fear or the complications that would come if their drug of choice was illegal? What would it really mean if, when they used their drug of choice, they could be arrested, or locked up, or face exclusion from the community? We'd like to invite people into a consideration of this.

Most of the people I know who use speed don't drink - they don't like alcohol. They don't like the way it makes them feel. They don't like feeling out of control, they don't like having a hangover the next day. Speed is their drug of choice. It would be nice if their choice could be just as respected as those people who drink alcohol but don't take speed.

How can we encourage people to respect other people's choices about which drugs they wish to use?

The first penalty for smoking in Turkey was to have the smoker parade through the streets with a pipe stem stuck through the nose. Later this penalty was increased to death. Despite the harshness of these penalties, smoking continued. Many people were executed until 1648, when a Sultan came to the throne who was himself a smoker. Turkey then changed to a country that profited through the trade of tobacco, spreading the drug throughout the Ottoman empire.

Tobacco use was introduced to Russia in the early seventeenth century. The period was a watershed in Russian history. Outside influences were becoming stronger and stronger, but were met with opposition from conservative forces inside the country. Chief among these were the clergy. The conservatives saw tobacco as one more aspect of Western influence, and through their actions incited prohibition in 1634. The initial penalty was whipping or torture, usually in public, repeat offenders being exiled to Siberia. When these measures were found to be unsuccessful, the death penalty was imposed. Use continued despite the harshness of these penalties. (White 1991, p.33)

So, some drugs are sanctioned, advertised and glorified, while on others war is declared. What are the implications of declaring war on drugs - which in reality means declaring war on the people who use those drugs? How did the drug laws convince us they were for our own good? How is declaring war on young users going to help them? How is a criminal record going to help them? How can workers ensure that the politics of drug use are not obscured in their conversations with young people around drugs?

Part Two: Deconstructing Dominant Ideas about Drug Use

Our responses to people who are using drugs are influenced by the dominant ideas about drug use in the broader culture. No matter how comfortable we are about drug use, even if we see it all the time, we exist in a society in which the use of certain drugs is looked upon negatively and to some extent our responses will be influenced by these dominant understandings. Drug use is a loaded topic - no matter how groovy we think we are.

In this section we have tried to demystify some of the common understandings about people who use drugs, and drug use itself. We hope that these explorations will assist people to be thoughtful about how they respond to their own and/or other people's drug use.

- *How can we have an awareness of what beliefs and attitudes inform our ideas about drug use?*
- *Where have these beliefs, attitudes come from?*
- *How do they influence our responses to people who use drugs?*
- *What are the effects of our responses?*
- *How can we notice what is a helpful effect and what isn't?*

These questions have guided us in the following explorations.

Deflating the tiresome idea of peer pressure

In discussions about young people who use drugs, the idea of peer pressure often seems to dominate. What does it mean that the term peer pressure is used to answer the question, 'Why do young people use drugs?' We think the term peer pressure is disqualifying of young people's culture and young people's community. It implies that young people aren't able to make their own decisions and that young people's friends are bad for them. This can break down a sense of community and can contribute to isolation. What does it mean that the term peer pressure is so widely used?

When young people are asked why they use drugs, they are not likely to say 'because I am a victim of peer pressure'. Even if being connected to a friendship group is part of the reason why they choose to take drugs, it is difficult but important to remember that drug use by young people is an informed decision made by weighing priorities, thinking things through and deciding upon a particular path.

It is true that when drugs are around and available, people will be more likely to be thinking about them. The choice is offered, but rarely is there direct pressure. Using drugs is a decision made by the young person. It is not forced upon them. Other people may not agree with the decision, or might not have made the same choices, but to deny that it is a decision is condescending.

Peer pressure, according to the *Mosaic* team, is an appalling term. Rather than telling young people that their friends aren't very good for them, there are other ways of understanding drug use. If workers resisted blaming other young people for drug use and instead began to look at the broader historical and political context of the use of drugs, what difference would this make?

Getting away from the idea of getting away

It is common to hear workers say to someone who is wanting to use less, that they've got to get away from their using friends. But if someone has been using a long time then these people may be their only friends. We wonder how young people are supposed to deal with getting off heroin if one of the steps is to get rid of their entire support network.

Sometimes a change of context may be needed, but if friends who are using are the only supportive network someone has, then to cut off from them may be counter-productive. Having friends through difficult times is important. What does it mean to deliberately break up the community and support network of people who are trying to stop using drugs?

Sometimes young people may need to move away from the people they know, but this needs to be their own decision. Workers need to take care not to impose their ideas in this area.

If workers push young people to 'get away' from their networks, they deny themselves access to the networks of information that young people depend upon. These networks, if used well, can be a resource. We need to find ways of using these networks rather than discarding them. Who would know what someone is struggling with better than their network who is also using? Who else would truly understand their experience?

Young people as victims

The idea that young people are victims of the drug culture, or victims of terrible drug-pusher characters, is also unhelpful. The logical conclusion of the myth around young people as victims is that unless you come in contact with a victimiser then you're not at risk and everything will be all right. We are told to look out for this situation or that situation, but that is not how it happens. Drug use isn't something that is inflicted upon you.

Beyond simple understandings of group identity

There also seems to be this idea that if young people have a group identity then they can't think separately, that they 'think in packs'. This is unhelpful for two reasons. If people identify as being part of a supportive and special group then that's a special thing, worth celebrating rather than problematising. Also, it would be much more helpful if workers could understand young people as individuals who are a part of a group rather than seeing them as either isolated individuals or part of a pack identity.

Hitting rock bottom

There seems to be a belief that 'you can't do anything' about people who are using drugs until they hit 'rock bottom'. There's a myth that cutting back doesn't work, that once you're a user you have to stop using completely in order to have any control over your life. These kind of ideas often become self-fulfilling and are very discouraging of people who have cut back and are happy with how they are using. Accepting people's individual truths about drug use is important. This either/or idea - you are either a user or you are not, you either take drugs or you don't, you're either screwed up or you're not, you're either one of us or you're one of them - is not helpful. How can we get away from this polarised view?

Distancing from people who are using

In trying to find ways to reduce the sense of isolation that happens around drug use, we've had a few questions to think through. What is it that separates people who are using drugs from their friends? Why is it that the distance happens? Because of the morality that surrounds drug use, there can be almost a sense of obligation to distance yourself from someone who is using drugs. It's as if to associate with someone who is using drugs is to 'condone' their using. It's as if you could catch something by association or as if by hanging out with them you are going to make it worse. This is pretty bizarre. It's not as if staying away from someone is going to make them stop using, but there seems to be an idea about loyalty to the 'real' person - the person who wasn't using drugs. It's as if shunning the person is an act of love.

How can we acknowledge that watching someone you care about start changing can be incredibly painful? How can we separate responses that come from a moral viewpoint from those that come from a different place - of 'I just can't stand it any more, I can't watch this any more'?

Erosion of trust

Young people are told not to trust their using friends, not to invite them over or they will steal everything. They are taught not to trust the information that they give each other. Young people are not invited to inform each other; in fact we are actively encouraged not to trust the knowledge we have acquired for ourselves. We are told that our information is likely to be inaccurate and we should ask someone who knows what they are talking about - someone professional. We wonder how conversations could be created that would help young people to protect trust between them. A young person's using network, which is really the family they have chosen, is realistically more likely to be helpful than a worker who has never used and hasn't educated themselves about the realities of young people's lives.

Even though we are told not to trust each other's information, it is our primary source of knowledge - especially around issues of drug use. People know how to seek out information from their friends.

Strip down identity and rebuild it

It's commonly believed that in order for someone to give up using drugs, they need to strip down the entire identity that they had as a user and create a new person. But this whole idea of stripping down doesn't honour history. There's no honouring of the richness of experience that people have gathered over the time of their using. History is seen only as damage and as the cause of what has gone wrong - it's because they had a miserable childhood, etc. There's a feeling that history must be erased. This is incredibly sad, because within those histories are all the amazing skills that people have acquired over years. These are the skills and experiences that will assist the person to take control of their using. If they want to stop using then there will be aspects of their history which will have helped them to get to that point. Reclaiming history also involves challenging the metaphor of 'wasted years' which is often used in relation to drug use. Instead of describing years as wasted, it might be much more constructive to explore that time for skills and knowledges that might be useful in the present.

Part Three: Alternative Stories about Young People and Drugs

Drugs as a way of surviving or sorting things out

There is an idea that when people use drugs they are somehow 'on hold' - avoiding facing the difficult issues in their lives. But for some people, drug use is not only a way of surviving but also a way of being able to *face* certain aspects of their lives. Drug use can be helpful at times in taking the edge off things and making them more manageable to think about. What would it mean for workers to understand that the detachment provided by drugs can be a positive thing? At other times, drugs can bring the issue to the forefront - especially when coming down. The alternative perspective offered by this can be helpful.

Celebration

In some circumstances, there are things to celebrate about drug use - including curiosity and a zest for life. There are people who use who are honestly happy, loving life, and are using because they love it, enjoy it. What would it mean to see curiosity, bravery and intellect as all a part of drug use (as opposed to seeing only recklessness and stupidity)? It is really complex trying to honour the curiosity and depth of experience related to drug use when many of us have lost people to isolation and overdose. How can we acknowledge the complexity? How can we acknowledge the positive intentions that may lead people to use drugs? How can we talk abut drug use without buying into the polarisation that either demonises or romanticises it?

Hopes and dreams

Many people seem to think that people who are using heavily have no hopes or dreams. There is an idea that they have become a blank, a mobile empty space, that there's nothing going on inside - no thoughts, no alternative ideas for the future. From the outside, it can look as if people who use a lot don't care if it kills them. But if this were true, why would they still be alive?

When people are using, of course they have dreams. If they are really stuck in it, if they are in the pits, it is only their dreams and hopes that keep them holding on at all. It is not possible to simply become a blank. Nothing can erase people that completely. Every day there are exceptions to the dominant drug story, there are times when people are in touch with their hopes and dreams.

Choice

It would be good if it could be acknowledged that young people make choices about drug use based on what they know. They are informed choices. Young people are generally aware of the effects of the choices they have made. It is important that workers are open to acknowledging and exploring with young people how they have made their choices, how they arrived at certain decisions and what those decisions mean to them. In this way, young people can be invited to think about how they've arrived at their decisions. If these conversations happen then young people are allowed to access their own history of being responsible. This can redress the messages of irresponsibility that are implied by the dominant ideas around drug use.

Drugs as avenues of pleasure

A dominant idea seems to be that people take drugs as a way of escaping from life. What would it mean to have some alternative ideas about this - to perhaps see drug use as an experience that people have chosen to take? People have many reasons for taking drugs - escape is one of them, but not necessarily the major one. People take drugs because it's fun, because of a sense of adventure. Or simply because they like the way they feel when they are using.

A history of protest

Drug use can also be about a history of protest. It may be a choice people have made to avoid another kind of experience, or to change their relationship with that experience.

Part Four: Workers' Attitudes to Drug Use

Because of the stigma and dominant ideas associated with illicit drug use, workers' attitudes may inadvertently reduce the possibilities for good conversations. Here we explore some of the ways in which this can occur.

Propaganda

One of the reasons young people have rejected traditional drug education is that they see it as biased, as propaganda. They think that they are being given only one side of the story because the agenda behind the education is clearly to stop them using drugs. (Cripps 1997, p.16)

Often workers approach work around drug use with the intention to stop the young person from using, even if this is not what the young person wants. Actually sorting out what the young person does want needs to be the place to start. We want to acknowledge that it can be hard for workers not to have the agenda to stop people using, because using drugs often isn't that great for your health, especially by the time you're seeing a worker. However, if the service is going to be accessible, it's important not to have different intentions than the young person.

Young people know more or less what they want from a worker. Workers can just ask them. Unless young people actually want to stop using, it's not going to do much good if workers come from a place of trying to make them stop. It shuts down the possibilities for a conversation. If workers take care not to impose their ideas and to keep in touch with what young people are wanting, then if the time comes when the young person wants to stop using, there will be a trust and a sense that the worker is listening to what the young person wants from them.

Credibility

People working with young people need to know the details about drug use, what people do, how they do it, down to the minute details. This is important so that when workers talk with young people they are comfortable with the topic. It's workers' responsibility to learn. Otherwise there is a huge credibility gap. Workers need to consult with young people and they also need to go and do their homework, to go to other agencies, to meet the people they are referring young people to.

Personal questions

Workers need to think through what their response will be when young people ask them, 'Have you ever used?' We acknowledge that this question can place workers in a complex position. Because of the stigma associated with drug use, and possible repercussions for workers, it is complicated to enter this conversation. Workers will have to find their own way through this one, but they are going to be asked, so it might be good to think it through beforehand so they are not flustered in their response.

Worry and panic

One of the things that clearly gets in the way of workers staying with the intentions of young people is when worry builds and they panic. This is pretty understandable, given the number of deaths around drug use, but it's important to find ways of dealing with worry and panic. Here are some ideas:

There are times when it makes sense to worry about someone's drug use. I start to worry when people are losing track of the things that are important to them. If I know someone and know what is important in their life and see that these things are slipping away, that's when I start getting really worried. But if I think they've got a focus, if they have an anchor, then their use doesn't worry me. They could use quite a lot and it wouldn't worry me, as long as they are clear that they aren't going to let it take over the things that are important. If someone doesn't have anything that they are living for, however, then they could be using not very much at all and still it would really worry me. If people don't have anything to keep them grounded, any anchoring, I worry.

If this worry starts to act, how can we make sure that it doesn't take us away from the person, or that it doesn't immobilise us? Even though there may be cause for worry, how can we respond in ways that don't separate us from the person that we are worried about? Sometimes in the past when I have been worried and approached people, they have just said that they're fine. Or they might get offended or defensive. I have tried to think of ways to respond to these situations. Here are some questions that I think might help:

- *How do I know that you will be all right?*

- *What can you do, and what can I do, to help me to understand that you will be all right?*

- *What are the things that make you know you are going to be all right? Could you share them with me? I might feel a whole lot safer about it all if I knew those things.*

Asking these sorts of questions might also help to build on the experiences, knowledges and skills that are going to assist the young person to reclaim or remain in control. They locate the worry outside of the person having a problem, and into 'What can we do about the fact that this is freaking me out?' It's deferring to their knowledges about their own life too.

Self protective strategies

It's important that workers be interested in what helps young people keep control of their drug use. Actually being interested in asking young people what helps them is a first step. One helpful question might be, 'In the times when you feel more in control about your drug use, what are the things that help you to have that control?'

The preservation of ritual

One of the things that young people have said helps them to stay in control is to reclaim rituals around their drug use. It's actually quite a radical thought for workers to talk about making drug use an occasion, because it could be seen as endorsement and workers could feel complicit. For some workers, asking questions like 'How does making a ritual of your drug-taking help?' could feel a bit too close to saying that taking drugs is a nice thing to do. But young people are saying that conversations about the preservation of ritual would be helpful.

Setting aside a time and place, making an occasion of it and taking care with who is around are all a part of preserving ritual around drug use.

A lot of people I have known over the years get the drug and rush to the nearest toilet block, or rush to wherever is closest for them to use, with no sense of ritual. Just to bring the drug home, and not go a hundred kilometres an hour to get there, to take your time, stop and get your cigarettes, your drink or whatever, get home and make it all nice, set it up - it all makes a difference. I know of someone who has set up an altar in their room. They go there, get their spoon, and do things slowly with a sense of ritual. This is so different from going to the toilet block and using a dirty needle. It keeps the drug use in a particular place and with care. It keeps the drug use within their life in an okay way.

Going home to an altar brings into the whole experience considerations of quality, care - not just quantity. It is honouring of a person's choice and it is setting an honourable context. This is taking a stand against ways of thinking which bring with them implications and invitations of shame and wrongdoing.

Due to the illegality of young people's drugs of choice, and moral judgments about our drug use, we need to take extra care, to use rituals, to reclaim the space and the meanings around our drug use. We're told that drug use is 'disgusting, horrible' and somehow we are too for 'doing it to ourselves'. These are the sorts of things we must resist. Creating rituals of care can turn this around.

For people who have developed a physiological need for a drug, and their use is out of control, reclaiming ritual can be a first step in reclaiming control. Just being able to have a shower and get dressed before taking the drug can make someone feel a little more in control. It gives a message to themselves that the drug use is a decision they are making, that they've actually thought it out beforehand, that they've made the effort to make it as nice a context as possible. To put in that little bit of extra time and effort also encourages safe using. It means the person is more likely to have the things they need to use safely - e.g. clean fits, sterile water, swabs, etc.

For drugs that are sanctioned by society, some of the rituals around their use still exist - like waiting until after Christmas dinner to get pissed! For those using drugs that are illegal, simple things like setting aside time, planning in advance and creating a good context for using all need to be reclaimed.

Whether or not this would be reinforcing of people's drug use is pretty irrelevant. Importantly, it would reinforce people's sense of taking responsibility for their own lives. If they then choose to continue to use or to stop, it is up to them.

Part Five: Things to Do Today / Hands-on Learning

Here are some ideas of things to do to make a start on self-education:

♦ Ring your local needle exchange - the AIDS Council is often a good one - and ask if someone can come into your workplace and give a talk.

♦ Or, go and visit your local needle exchange. Go in, sit around for a while, get used to the atmosphere, ask lots of questions.

♦ Unpack a needle. Learn how to use it. Learn how to dispose of it.

♦ Photocopy pages of this resource, distribute it to all the workers in your workplace and then put it on the agenda for discussion at your next staff meeting. Talk about where people might be struggling in their conversations around drug use and possible ways forward.

♦ Seek out pamphlets and information kits so that you can pass them on to the people who consult with you. There are some really good ones around. Try your local needle exchange, AIDS Council or Drug and Alcohol Information Service. Some of the areas that are important to know about include:

- overdoses: what they are, what causes them, what to do if one occurs, how to minimise the risk

- methadone programs

- vein maintenance

- information on all the different drugs - not just the horror stories but the good things too!

- information about HIV/AIDS and Hep C

♦ Make copies and share this resource with the young people in your life.

Do you want more information?

If you wish to seek out more information on this topic, please contact us c/- Dulwich Centre. We are currently working on another resource - this one will be produced for young people. We are also available to speak with people and organisations about the issue of drug use if you wish to take the conversation further.

Copies of *Mosaic* are available for $5 plus postage (donations are also most welcome!). All sales contribute to further *Mosaic* projects. Other sections of *Mosaic* include:

• background

• cultural histories of drug use

• responding to drug related deaths

• a wish-list - what services could be like

• examples of funky services

• a mother's perspective

• a view from the troops in the drug war (an interview with Bernie Morgan, senior Sergeant of the Hindley St Police Force)

- From Mr Sin to Mr Big: A History of Australian Drug Laws (a review)
- reflections from workers

Note

1. Penni & Paul can be contacted c/- Dulwich Centre, 345 Carrington St, Adelaide 5000, South Australia.

References

Cripps, C. 1997: 'Workers with Attitude', *Druglink,* May/June, p.15.

White, J.M 1991: *Drug Dependence.* Englewood Cliffs, New Jersey: Prentice Hall.

Day Three

14.

Documents and treasures, Power To Our Journeys

by

Sue, Mem & Veronica[1]

Power To Our Journeys was formed four years ago when a number of women who either currently struggle with hearing voices, or have heard voices in the past, came together to share their knowledges and skills and to challenge conventional ideas about mental health issues. In this keynote address, Sue, Mem and Veronika shared some of the discoveries that they have found along the way.

Hullo. Let us introduce ourselves. We are Mem, Veronika and Sue from the group Power To Our Journeys. We are part of a group of women who either currently or in the past have experienced hearing voices. These are the sort of voices that try to disempower us. These are the sort of voices that use harassment, denigration, and general name-calling, and that can become a force of tyranny. These are the sort of voices that can shut us in and isolate us from the world, and that can ruin our lives.

We come together as members of the Power To Our Journeys group to share our knowledges and skills, to support each other on our journeys through life, and to take a stand together to expand our lives from the small existence that the voices want to force on us. Not only do we come together as a group in these activities, but we are connected to many people around the world with whom we share our knowledges about reclaiming our lives from the voices. Along the way we have been supported by and linked with the Community Mental Health Project Team of the Dulwich Centre. The people of this team walk with us in solidarity and help us to make stands against the voices and to further develop strategies for reclaiming our lives.

One of the strategies that we use is to put together documents that provide an exposé on the operations of the voices, including the tactics of power that they use in their efforts to get the upperhand in our lives. These documents also provide an account of the knowledges and skills that we have developed and that are at our disposal to use to disempower the voices. We name these accounts of our knowledges and skills as documents because the name carries authority in our culture. The documentation of events is seen as a declaration of fact. Others have at times documented our lives in ways that are disrespectful, and because of this the voices have assumed more authority. This is why we need something strong, like our own documents, to stick it to the voices.

Today we would like to share with you a video of a conversation that we had about what these documents mean to us and what they do for our lives. In this conversation, we also talk about other treasures that have been important to us and which contribute to our 'backpack of tools' which we use to strengthen us and de-power the voices. As part of this we will be talking about the bundle of sticks that were sent to us from the people in Malawi, a small poor and landlocked country in central Africa. These people are struggling with a different tyranny - HIV infection at catastrophic levels. The sticks were sent in a gesture of solidarity in response to gifts of Power To Our Journeys T-shirts that we sent to Malawi.

In our preparation for this presentation we have had discussions about what it means to be sharing our lives and our journeys in such a public way here today, with predictions that the voices could subject us to a backlash. We also talked about not wanting to feel 'exposed' in this forum in an unequal way. We are very aware of stigma in society and have even at times stigmatised and marginalised ourselves. Not wanting to experience more of this here, we want you to understand that the experiences that we are sharing with you today do not represent the totality of our lives. We have all had experiences of other people and systems defining us. We are not making ourselves available for more of this - we are too busy living and loving. The terms by which we wish to be defined are: artist, singer, dancer, poet, musician, writer, activist, carer, kite-flyer and lace-maker.

For us to name stigma and marginalisation and to make it clear that we do not want to be named in the terms of stigma and marginalisation, unwinds the knot that we have in our stomachs in going public and allows us to be free to be who we are at this meeting - to be all that we are.

Before we share with you the video-tape of our conversations about documents and treasures, we would like to invite you to join in an equal dialogue that will challenge the 'them' and 'us' experience that sometimes comes from one-sided disclosures. This will make us less vulnerable to the backlash from the voices that we could experience in speaking out in this way. We would like you all right now to think of a time when you were feeling stressed out and, because of this, feeling isolated, full of self-doubt and lost, and under these circumstances losing touch with the knowledges and skills of living that are familiar to you. After reflecting on this, we would like you to then talk to the person sitting alongside of you for a few minutes about what worked for you in reclaiming these knowledges and skills of living in a way that made it possible for you to take some action, to come out of the wilderness. Who knows, perhaps you have also found documents useful at these times.

[Time was then given for people to complete the exercise.]

In some ways this video we're about to show feels like past tense. Since this video-tape was made, our lives have moved forward and we could tell you lots of wonderful stories about the new territories that we have charted, and about courageous steps that we have all taken.

But, for now, here is the video.

Talking about documents

Sue: I just adore the documents! Sometimes they seem like a life-line to myself - does that make sense? I have an image that represents to me the times in my life when I am lost. I can see myself floating out in the sea in a storm without an anchor, or a line, or an oar. Having the documents is like having an anchor, or an oar. They mean I can either stay put where I am, or I can row. They are tools with which I can take action. They remind me of who I am. At the same time, they also put out there what the voices are and what their tactics are. Sometimes I've used the documents as a kind of checklist to look back over and see that I've been in this place before. I go back over the documents and it's almost like they give me a charge inside that says, 'I actually did this, I got through this before and I can get through this again'.

Mem: It's a bit of a rush ...

Sue: Yeah. So you know what I mean? It is like a rush of confidence - 'I can do this'. It's a reminder that what I'm dealing with are the tactics of the voices and that really helps to shut the voices up. The documents are tangible things that I can hold in my hand. I can read them many, many times. Sometimes through the reading I can tune out. The documents are like a mirror that kind of outwits the voices, takes the wind out of their puffed-up sails and actually puffs me up! They give me confidence.

Veronika: I like to go back over the documents because they give me a sense of history. Some of the voices have been around for a long time and the documents let me know how I have dealt with them over years. The documents we write are very positive. I remember writing one after I went and saw a film. It was a Buddhist film showing at Buddha House. After I saw it I had five days of quiet. Five days of no voices. I couldn't believe it myself. I told the doctor and she was shocked. She said, 'Oh, alright' and told me not to go back to Buddha House! Maybe she was a little threatened! Something helped, that's for sure. [laughter] Anyway, after that I wrote a document called 'Five days of quiet'. Later, I was going over my documents one day and while I was reading this particular document one of the voices said, 'Five days quiet?' and I explained what happened and then the voice went, 'Well, who was I talking to for five days?' [extended laughter]

Sue: The voice said that?! [more laughter]

Veronika: Yeah, isn't that fantastic! All my documents are very positive so I can use them when I am down, when I need hope. The documents pinpoint things that bring hope. There are a couple that focus on things I'm thankful about. I've coloured in some mandalas and decorated the documents with them, put them in my little document book. The documents have been very important and useful for me.

Mem: The documents were really powerful for me in the beginning. I was so unwell at the time. In the sessions we would have, we'd make these points and write them down, and afterwards when I re-read them it would be suddenly like, 'Oh, this sounds like a real person, there's a person here'. For ages their significance was at that level. They were a reality check - 'Maybe I *did* do that'. Reading them through meant that I had a sense of being real, being the centre of all these energies. It took me a long time to sort of cotton on to this. After I read documents, I would know for certain that I was this particular person because I had these thoughts and feelings. There was a powerful sense of affirmation - no matter how low or what a strange place I was in, these documents were affirming me. They reassured me that I could be in the world. I found them very healing.

Often I get to some point and I know that I have struggled with this particular thing before. I think to myself now, 'What the hell was that? What situation have we talked about this sort of thing?' And in time it comes back. I recall the particular document, the particular conversation. I have internalised the documents in some way and that's given me strength. This was so important early on when I couldn't even get out of my house. Looking back, I can see the progression I took, and reading the documents was an important part of. Reading them was like affirming the self. They made me realise that I didn't have to be constricted to the house. No-one had ever suggested that to me before. Each time I read the documents, it was like they told me suggestions that no-one else had ever said. It brought a whole different way of thinking about things.

Gradually I turned my head round. There was a sense of Merrim in the documents, a sense of Mem, and that I was okay, and that I would get through this. After I started taking the tablets and having therapy, then the voices just disappeared. I still had to work out a lot of things for myself, though, that they (the voices) had been telling me about - like what to do, what to wear, when to wash, when to listen to the radio, all that sort of stuff. It was quite hard at first, working that all out. Where once I was having chats with the voices, now I started having a little chat with myself. I began to have different ongoing internal dialogues and this was a way of replacing the voices that's healing for me.

Talking about treasures - the bundle of sticks from Malawi

During this part of the conversation, Sue, Mem and Veronika passed around the bundle of sticks that were sent to Power To Our Journeys from the CARE Counsellors of Malawi.[2]

Sue: Sometimes when I'm in stressful situations and the voices are playing up, having the sticks next to me is really significant. They make me think of the people of Malawi overcoming enormous obstacles in their battles with HIV/AIDS, and they give me courage to keep going. I get strength from them and they shrink things so that they become more manageable. They remind me that when you're up against something very big then it's important to take things just one step at a time. They reconnect me to the importance of every little thing - how every small stick is important because it is together that we are strong.

Mem: Their naturalness is important to me. Isn't the tree these sticks have come from special in some way?

Sue: Yes, they are from trees that the Malawian people understand as sacred.

Mem: When I am holding them, I have a sense of their ancientness. I feel an ancientness in the heart when I hold them. They feel years and years old, and there is something about that which brings a sense of dignity and respect for culture.

Sue: I like that - the sense of dignity - that comes from holding them. Especially as in so many of our experiences our dignity has been ignored ...

Mem: ... and stripped from us. To think that these people in Malawi should be concerned or interested in our struggle as to give us these sticks as a present gives me strength.

Veronika: It brings me back to the thought of a joint struggle. Their struggle is different than ours, I can only try to imagine what they have experienced, but they've brought us together with this gift. They've put their names and addresses on the sticks too, so if you wanted to write to anyone then you could. The distance is what astounds me, just how far away they are and yet ... well, I think about them a lot, every time I see the sticks ... and I feel I am not alone.

Fighting AIDS is a lot more final than what I'm struggling with in relation to hearing voices. And yet they keep their spirit, and they still want to give. They organised to give us these sticks and also a sarong. To give to us when we in this country have everything, it's an inspiration. These sticks are a source of inspiration.

Mem: We gave them a present, too, didn't we? - the T-shirts.

Sue: Yes. And we sent them the Power To Our Journeys song which they learnt to sing too, and then they sent us a song as well. For me, these sticks are a powerful survival tool to carry around in my backpack. They're powerful for the spirit. When the voices are having a go at me, or life's kind of getting tough, having these treasures is so tangible. I can put my hand on them and hold them or literally carry them around for a day in my backpack. When things get a bit scary, I can just open up the backpack and say 'Oh, there they are'.

I've taken these sticks and the sarong to many places where I've been full of fear, where I've known I could be overwhelmed with fear. I might be at a course or something, and when the voices are having a go at me, I open up my backpack, stick my hand in there and just grab the sticks, or just look at them, and they remind me that I'm who I am. That might not seem to make sense but they give me courage and they remind me of my connection with people. Doctors or workshop leaders, or teachers, or whoever it is I am having to deal with at the time, may not know anything about me. Just having the sticks is like a secret. It's a secret connection to this group

(Power To Our Journeys), the community mental health project, and the people in Malawi. It changes my perspective on things.

Mem: Who would have thought a bundle of sticks could have such meaning!

Sue: I feel honoured to feel their enormous energy - they are like my secret weapon! [laughter]

Mem: Look out, here comes Super Sticks! It's not like that they're materially significant or wealthy, they're just little sticks, but they have so much meaning, it's as though they're a gold nugget. Do you know what I mean?

Sue: Yeah, I do.

The Power to Our Journeys Song

To finish up the presentation, Sue, Mem and Veronika invited all the conference participants to join them in a rendition of the Power To Our Journeys song, which, they described, is in celebration of all our journeys.

Power to our journeys
A song by Sue & David

A journey of a thousand miles begins with one step
We're coming together now, we're talking 'bout respect
It shouldn't be too much to ask to listen and to learn
To fill the libraries with strategies that work

Chorus: *There is power to our journeys*
           There is hope in this room
           Voices to be heard
           And stories to be told

What could these be that we've planted here today?
What could these be that we're watering so carefully?
Could they be friendships, something so sacred, yet so simple?
Could they be friend 'ships' to sail?

Chorus

As we tell our stories, we remember friends on similar journeys;
We take their hands, and join them in rage
And join them in sorrow, and join them in hopefulness

Chorus

Well we're trying to get it together,
But, together we have it all
Well, we're trying to get it together
But, together we have it all
We're silently boiling over, we're silently boiling over
We're silently boiling over, we're silently boiling over

Chorus

There is power to our journeys

Notes

1. Sue, Mem & Veronica can be contacted c/- Dulwich Centre, 345 Carrington St, Adelaide 5000, South Australia.

2. The bundle of sticks was given to Power To Our Journeys in response to gifts of T-shirts and the singing of the Power To Our Journeys song. The bundle of sticks represents a traditional Malawian story. It is a story that speaks of the power of standing together in the face of problems. *A stick on its own can be easily broken. But if you take sticks from the magic trees and place them in a bundle, the bundle becomes very strong, so strong that you cannot break it.*

   For further explorations of the ways in which this story is used by the CARE Counsellors of Malawi in their work with issues of HIV/AIDS see '*Pang'ono pang'ono ndi mtolo* - little by little we make a bundle: the work of the CARE Counsellors of Malawi & Yvonne Sliep', in *Introducing Narrative Therapy: A collection of practice-based writings,* (eds) Cheryl White & David Denborough, Dulwich Centre Publications, Adelaide (1998).

15.

Bridging the gap:
Conversations about mental illness experiences

by

Gaye Stockell & Marilyn O'Neill [1]

Over the years in which we have worked within community mental health services, we have had the privilege to hear many stories from people about their experiences of psychosis and their encounters with the services established to assist them. Many of these people have spoken of their own journey with particular purpose - to enable others to come to know what is useful and not useful in relation to responding to mental illness, in the hope that more helpful approaches can be generated. Many of the people who have shared their ideas with us have also hoped that their experience would be understood and appreciated differently to the way they found it was commonly viewed.

Not only have the ideas of the many people who have talked with us about these issues inspired our work with others, they have also been personally encouraging. It has become possible together to develop different, more helpful and enabling views of the experience of mental illness. This has challenged the traditional practices that we are often trained to work with, and has resulted in the evolution of a never-ending position of questioning that regularly informs our conversations with other workers in health and community services.

Today we wish to speak of the ideas of just one collection of people with whom we have been able to consult. The 'Bridging the Gap' Project was initiated by the Northern Sydney Community Mental Health Services[2] and involved consultations with people with experiences of mental illness, their families, workers in the mental health services and service managers. The idea of the project was to conduct a collaborative/narrative/co-research conversation with the people involved in the provision and utilisation of a large mental health service. The idea was very appealing to us, as it was a chance to formally gather together some of the wisdoms about mental illness we knew these people had, and to circulate them amongst those we talked with, as well as to a wider audience.

Establishing the project

To establish the project, we thought it was important to invite all parties to participate, that is, those people who have had and continue to have the direct experience of mental illness; families and friends associated with them; mental health workers and service managers. We also believed that using a narrative approach as the consultative process would enable us to engage in conversations that would:

- assist in separating problems from people;
- help us work together at exploring dilemmas;
- uncover positive information about useful ways of viewing and dealing with dilemmas, especially when an overwhelming negative experience has meant those alternatives have been overlooked;
- take a political position that would validate individual experiences and provide an understanding of the powerful forces operating in people's lives;
- acknowledge the importance of context and connectedness;
- offer the possibility of discovering directions people prefer for their lives and relationships.

Planning consultations

The initial part of the project was to establish the consultative process and an accountability mechanism for that process. We invited representatives from each of the nominated consultative groups to attend discussions aimed at exploring everyone's hopes for the project.

At the first meeting, we met up with people who have had the direct experience of mental illness, and members of their family. We introduced the ideas incorporated in narrative approaches to conversations. We spoke about David Epston's ideas on co-research and invited the participants to give their thoughts and opinions.

Curiosity and enthusiasm for working in partnership were apparent. Participants identified a number of difficulties they had personally experienced in previous interactions. Hopes emerged for a collaborative exploration that would allow us to work together exploring the unique and common difficulties experienced.

The metaphor of 'the gap'

In these initial consultations, one participant introduced the metaphor of 'the gap'. She explained 'the gap' as something that occurs as a result of differing perspectives. She said that, when an event occurs as a result of mental illness, each concerned witness to that event becomes like a 'mirror'. The 'mirror' is placed at a certain angle and then reflects particular aspects of the event. Each person knows their reflection is the correct one, because it is in their mirror. However, each reflection presents a slightly different angle on the event and it is possible from different angles to construe different meanings.

This metaphor represented for the group an understanding of people's differing perspectives on the same event. The group thought people often relied on the one interpretation of the experience to the exclusion of other reflections. This raised questions such as: What other interpretations might be possible if the mirrors were all used in the process of developing a more complete picture?

The group encouraged us to embark on the project. They were keen to have the ideas of all groups, including workers and management, gathered and cross-fertilised as a basis for future co-operative action. Their ideas and questions were taken as a guide for further collaborative consultations. Our hopes were to include the perspectives of all parties. We decided to call this project 'Bridging the Gap'.

Project Consultations

Individual consultations

Three people who experienced mental illness and who had heard about the project offered to contribute their ideas. Their contributions were extremely valuable.

Raymond[3] a member of the rehabilitation service, gave us feedback on the positive effects narrative conversations have had on his life. He said that this style of conversation had allowed him to shift his relationship with his illness. He said that after these conversations 'the illness started to take care of itself'. He could 'treat it just as any other illness', and he was then 'free to do ordinary things like getting enough sleep, learning to do what worked best' and 'dealing with the problem of carrying tension'. Raymond told us the technique of the narrative conversations had allowed him to name problems and separate them from himself. This had freed his thinking and actions so that he was no longer immobilised.

Alan[4] raised with us the dilemmas of not knowing about members' experience of the service and how various decisions were made. The practices occurring in hospitals were of serious concern to Alan. He was particularly troubled by his observations that the least experienced medical practitioners were often the ones given the care of the people most troubled by mental illness. He also believed that the most experienced dealt with the least troubled. Alan believed that by pooling his thoughts with others who have had experiences of mental illness, and then pooling that expertise with that of workers, we might develop some useful ideas.

A third consultation with Tony[5] highlighted dilemmas arising from 'being told what to do'. Tony related his experience of his time in a residential setting and of the experiences of his friends who were still living in that setting.

He believed support was important, but he had developed ideas about what was and wasn't helpful. He said it wasn't useful to be told 'how to live your life', the ways 'you should do this'. He said it was useful to be consulted and supported in relation to your own ideas about what was good for you. He recognised the practical difficulties this might impose on workers, but felt strongly that it was an important consideration for rehabilitation and human rights.

Family consultations

Other consultations for the project took place with five families. The focus of these meetings was the ways in which family members were recognising the effects that mental illness was having on their lives, their relationships with others and with the wider community. The discussions in all families generated a greater understanding and appreciation of working together. Families spoke of how the experience of 'being on the same team' allowed their dilemmas to be dealt with. These family meetings gave all of us a sense of being a participant in a bridging of 'the gap'. Family members spoke of how the conversations enabled them to see difficult situations from other angles.

Worker consultations

The next phase of the project involved responding to an invitation from one of the teams of workers to join in an exploration of some of the difficulties they were having with their work. Team members nominated 'busyness' as a shared problem. Busyness was seen by them as having a major influence on their work practices. Although some saw busyness as giving them a sense of competence in crisis for the most part, it was recognised as establishing a culture of 'fire fighting'. It invited 'an anxious view of clients as unmade beds' and encouraged workers, regardless of profession, to develop 'a super-nurse syndrome'.

The team identified that the problems they experienced were related to gaps between rhetoric and reality. They spoke of perceived expectations held by management versus everyday possibilities, and the difference between their expectations as workers and the expectations of those people who accessed their services. The team considered how they might prevent busyness from robbing them of the opportunity for helpful reflections on their work. We evolved the following questions for consideration:

- How might we convey the dilemmas and richness of our work and break from the isolation that lack of understanding often creates?

- How might we convey the nature of the work to management in ways that might address the restraints of upward accountability?

- How do we do justice to the team's ideas and 'not just mutter on'?

A second consultation with workers took place with the rehabilitation service. They also wanted to address dilemmas related to their work practices and to explore the gaps created between people in the psychiatric arena. They said the gaps often related to the differing expectations people had of the service, and the varying values sometimes given to different aspects of the service. They recognised, however, the significance for them, as a team, of having together embraced a narrative approach to their work. It had opened up possibilities of more clearly naming and dealing with the concerns people have with mental illness.

Using the narrative process, the team generated a number of questions that related to traditional recreation activities and rehabilitation programs:

- Whose purposes do these activities mostly serve?

- What meaning does an everyday activity have for a person if it is structured and supervised by health professionals?

- How do people come to know themselves when the activities in their life are focused on deficits and inabilities?

- How might we as workers assist people to know themselves as members of the community?

- How can we invite the wider community to recognise the membership of people whose lives are troubled by the effects of mental illness?

- How can workers free themselves of traditional expectations to 'do for' others and instead move into the position of 'support with'?

- How can we assist people who, as a result of institutionalised practices, have been robbed of helpful ways of knowing themselves?

The team had some ideas as to answering these questions but valued continuing the questioning process as a means of avoiding the trap of replicating traditionally unhelpful practices of the past.

Women's group consultation

Further consultation then took place with a group of women who had been meeting regularly in a 'Worthy of Discussion Group'[6]. These conversations provided us with these women's thoughts on managing psychosis. They said that:

- Help from others is best if it is firm but gentle and loving. It's best if it comes from someone you know.
- At times you need to repeat things frequently and firmly - the psychosis can get in the way of you hearing things.
- Allow us to talk - listen to us.
- The worst thing is someone who is impatient, angry, intolerant, unwilling to learn. It makes you sicker.
- It is useful to keep away from other people's negativity.
- Try not to be fearful of it [mental illness]. Fear makes the experience even more negative.
- What helps is to be your own best friend - love yourself.

These women also spoke of some positive messages you can give yourself.

The women also gave us feedback on their experience of narrative conversations in the 'Worthy of Discussion Group'. They said:

- The narrative questions help me build up a picture of what's going on for me. Over time, that has helped me change my perspective.
- You can shrink from the task of changing. These narrative conversations challenge you to grow out of the sick feeling.

- Coming to the group is an assault on isolation; it was easier to stick to isolation before.

Multiple family meetings

Our next series of meetings was with a group of families who had recently had their first encounter with mental illness. From these meetings, we gathered a great diversity of thoughts and ideas. We hope we have been able to do justice in this report to the richness of the conversations.

Encounters with mental illness

The families spoke about their first encounter with mental illness in the following ways:

- You feel like you've been hit by a bus.
- You're in a state of shock at hearing the illness named.
- You're overwhelmed ... feel helpless and guilty.
- It alters the focus of your life.
- Despair.
- Mental illness made me think about the person all of the time.
- When you first encounter mental illness, you feel very alone. You see other families at the hospital, etc., but you don't get to speak to them.

Isolation

Isolation was a common theme and was described in the following ways:
- It's like being in the dark.
- It separates you from the person.

Challenges

Families described problems with communication and issues of responsibility as significant challenges. Fear and anger were also talked about and were thought by the families to widen the gap between family members.

'Shoulds'

Family members talked about the 'shoulds'. They said they found themselves:

- responding to other people's 'shoulds';
- being pushed for change that could be reached;
- being told that one is over-involved and should back off;

They said that these were all unhelpful situations.

Unhelpful practices

Families identified practices they recognised as blocking them from being helpful members of their relative's team. Practices they named included:

- those that conveyed worker's sense of busyness and burden;
- attitudes of defensiveness, mistrust and secrecy;
- and practices that established an inconsistency of expectations, for example, that the family would be able to manage a demanding crisis (because they had been through it before) while at the same time needing a basic 'how to do it' manual on everyday living (because their family member might one day be in crisis).

Family strategies for bridging gaps

We asked families what ideas they had for dealing with the negative effects of mental illness. They said what was important to them was:

- Recognising what it is - identifying things.
- Knowing that maintaining the status quo doesn't work.
- Negotiating reality.
- Slowing down the pace.
- Finding self-care activities and ways to feel positive about yourself.

The families had some specific ideas about psychosis. It was felt that:

- You need to take a stand against psychosis.
- It is good to talk openly about it when the person is experiencing the

psychosis, in ways that do not deny the person's experience. This means you know what is going on. You often get to hear about things and have an understanding that is not available to health professionals.

The families' ideas for opening up communication included:

• Reclaiming the past experiences of helpful communication.

• Being able to stay non-reactive and non-judgemental.

In speaking about issues of responsibility, family members thought it useful to ask questions that invite a reflection on the impact that actions and thoughts have on others.

In speaking about their ideas on their relationship with mental health services, one group spoke about the importance of maps: 'You don't have to know everything about mental illness, but a map with guideposts would be helpful. Not a road to follow, because every road is different. Just some guideposts that can offer you different turns and routes.'

Inclusion

Families strongly favoured an approach that included them from the onset. They found that when they were all able to work together as a team, relationships became more natural and the pace more manageable. The idea of consultative teamwork was predicted to offer the evolution of more useful practical knowledge, and fewer occasions of crisis, fear and isolation for all concerned.

Final project meeting

A final meeting was organised to give a report on the project to all six participating consultative groups. We also planned that this meeting would enable a cross-fertilisation of the ideas and experiences of those involved as consultants to the project. Our hopes were that this cross-fertilisation would honour and publicise the special knowledge all groups had acquired in dealing with mental illness, and that this might contribute to a bridging of the gaps. With this in mind, we called together members of all the different consultation groups.

Before we could simply report back on the consultations, however, we needed to ask the group of managers and workers who were unable to attend previous meetings because of busyness to consider some of the questions that the other groups had discussed. These questions asked people to consider the impact of mental illness on their own lives and work. We also asked the managers to offer their ideas about dealing with the negative effects of mental illness.

In order to address some of the issues of power and privilege that might arise from such a meeting (in which service providers, managers, those accessing the services and family members of those accessing the services were present), those group participants who had already considered the questions became questioners and scribes as the workers and managers gave their answers and reflections.

The mental health workers gave diverse responses to the question about the effects of mental illness on their lives and roles. Some workers had trouble thinking of the ways in which mental illness affected them. Some saw it totally ruling their work role. They discussed the positive and negative effects of mental illness on their work practices.

In reflecting on the workers' discussion, the scribes wondered what it would be like for workers when the mental illness was ebbing if they only felt particularly purposeful at times of crisis. Another scribe wondered about the idea that mental illness required workers to see the funny side of things. She reflected on the effects on the possible implications for those on whom the jokes rested.

The scribes noted the practical and purposeful ideas which workers brought to their discussions about taking a stand against the negative effects of mental illness. They noted their desire to work co-operatively and fully. The scribes' final comments related to the need for political and community responses, and for the development of more networking. They asked the question: 'Who will attend to these needs?'

At the conclusion of the meeting, there was enthusiasm for circulating further the ideas that had been discussed, for continuing the consultative process, and for publishing the project.

To end the meeting, we invited everyone gathered to reflect on: 'In light of the experience of this collaborative consultation, what possibilities might now exist for all involved in mental health services?'

Reflections

The presentation of these ideas at the Inaugural Dulwich Centre Publications' Narrative Therapy and Community Work Conference addressed an unmet hope that we and participants had held for this project - that others in the world of health and welfare and in the wider community would get to reflect on these views and knowledges. It enabled the experiences of the people who contributed their ideas about mental illness to the co-research project to stand with the women of the Power to Our Journeys Group, with whom we co-presented.

Notes

1. Gaye & Marilyn can be contacted c/- 314 Nicholson St, Crows Nest NSW 2065, Australia, phone (61-2) 9966 5966, fax: (61-2) 9966 0618.

2. The project was supported by the Director of this service, Alan Rosen, with the encouragement and consultation of David Epston.

3. Raymond wanted to be known only by his first name.

4. This is a pseudonym.

5. This is a pseudonym.

6. O'Neill, M. & Stockell, G. 1991: 'Worthy of Discussion: Collaborative group therapy.' *Australia & New Zealand Journal of Family Therapy*, 12(4).

16.

Co-research:
The making of an alternative knowledge

by

David Epston[1]

Co-research was a term I concocted in a very specific set of circumstances to describe to myself and others a practice at considerable variance to 'family therapy' of the late 1970s. Around that time, I began a very valued association with Dr Innes Asher, a respiratory physician at the Department of Paediatrics, University of Auckland. We began to collaborate around those children, adolescents and their families who were suffering the experience of life-threatening, chronic and often disabling asthma. Such suffering, as I was to learn, had no 'voice', no vocabulary and no place in the biomedical discourses. If anything, it was rigorously excluded. A 'good patient' was calm and enduring, and such manners were certainly expected of the family members concerned. But such a life-threatening asthma, referred to as 'brittle', could happen almost any time day or night, seemingly with little or no warning.

Ronny's story

The first young man I was to meet was twelve. By then, Ronny had suffered numerous respiratory arrests, each one threatening his life, following his first arrest on the occasion of his eleventh birthday party. What made matters grave was that he had also started cardiac arresting, although his heart according to the cardiologists was 'as strong as an ox'. His parents, who lived a 60-kilometre ambulance ride away from the Children's Hospital, could only submit to two sleepless nights before Ronny insisted on returning to the hospital. He was so concerned for his parents' well-being. Such was the hospital's concern for him that a suggestion had been floated that he live in intensive care. Everyone worried that he did not have long to live.

In fact, I noted when talking to hospital staff involved in his intimate care, they would betray their fears for him without even knowing it - a slight tremor at the mention of his name. However, as I canvassed everyone, a nurse on the night shift told me a story I will never forget. She has to remain nameless because by the time I realised its significance, she was lost in the regular rotation of nurses throughout the hospital.

One night when Ronny rang his night alarm, she raced to his bedside and found him in great distress. This usually signalled an arrest. However, at the same time, she was summoned to another alert which had priority and there were no other nurses available at that moment. She had to leave Ronny. She called upon all her courage, looked Ronny straight in the eye and shouted 'STOP IT!' They were both stunned by the fact that his distress immediately abated and she was safely able to leave him. Although this had been duly noted in his 'medical chart', it went unattended to, a mere curiosity. This incident, considered at some length, became foundational to a 'courage practice' that was trialed with consent under the most hazardous conditions. I was permitted, in a manner of speaking, to give him asthma attacks. I had noticed that my mere mentioning of the word 'cough(ing)' was more than sufficient to bring on extreme wheezing. With Dr Louise Webster on medical guard behind Ronny and me, we commenced to 'arrest arrests'. For example, when he was mildly distressed, I would offer him a handful of coins and ask him to pick one. I would then ask him to read the date on it. My next question, 'Ronny, what was it like to arrest an arrest?', was met by great bemusement. On each trial, I allowed his wheezing to worsen until the final occasion. He began to lapse into semi-consciousness, turning an awful blue. Dates on coins were no longer of any interest. I seized his hand, gently squeezing it, repeating 'Feel my strength passing into your mind and body'. I sensed I was losing him at the same time as my strength was running out. With my last gasp, I fiercely squeezed his hand and shouted 'STOP IT!' To everyone's amazement, he did exactly that and stopped it. Obviously confused, as a full day had been dedicated to 'arresting arrests', he jumped to full attention and rushed out of the room like the Mad Hatter saying that he was late for an important x-ray date. The nurses from the nearby nursing station rushed in, seeking information. Louise shouted, 'He did it!' and, like wildfire, the news spread around the ward and beyond.

Ronny was soon able to return home to live, had only one further hospitalisation, and was able to resume a normal life. Innes and I have kept in touch with him one way and another ever since.

Acknowledging alternative knowledges

This experience with Ronny was formative in convincing me there were 'alternative knowledges' to the more conventional treatments for which Ronny had exhausted each and every possibility. What was particularly significant was where one might seek such knowledges - the metaphorical space created through an externalising conversation between the person/family/carers *and* the illness/disability.

Family therapy theory and practice in the late 1970s and early 1980s had also considered this, but I found them at worst 'family-blaming' and at best 'family suspicious'. Lyman Wynne summed up this state of affairs in 1992:

> *The family system explanations of illness can be regarded as an alternative version of the societal and traumatic life-event interpretations of illness. In each of these versions, not the individual but a larger social unit (family or society) is viewed as 'disturbing' or 'sick'. The hypothesis is that family systems are causative in generating or maintaining symptoms provided much of the impetus for starting the field of family therapy.* (Wynne, Shields & Sirkin 1992, p.13)

Concerning life-threatening asthma whereby family members had been involved in numerous life-saving incidents, either directly by administering CPR or indirectly by calling ambulance or intensive-care services, for me to operate on a family-suspicious basis seemed a grotesque travesty of benevolence, let alone a professional practice of therapy. I became determined to find an alternative frame of reference so I might meet these people with compassion rather than suspicion. First of all, I took 'suffering' to be the designated 'problem'. And by doing so, 'suffering' more or less became everyone's problem. And such suffering was beyond the scale of anything I had known close up. Unfortunately, there was more to come.

From empathy to ethnography

In the late 1980s, I felt I had no choice whatsoever but to further this endeavour to find an alternative when I met the membership of the Dystrophic Epidermolysis Bullosa Research Association. Although this is retrospective, I believe I got the word 'research' from sheer plagiarism. When I was first contacted by a colleague, Nick Birchall, a paediatric dermatologist, I recall being at pains to first learn how to pronounce it and then find out what in the world 'DEB', as it is known, was. He informed me it was a very rare genetic disorder variably affecting around 70 individuals in New Zealand. What I did remember most vividly was his description of a missing gene that metaphorically meant that it was like concrete without reinforcing steel. Without such reinforcement, the skin is extremely vulnerable to blistering or rupture at the slightest pressure or touch. The pain associated with this was so excruciating that lancing by razor blade is the only means of relief. Because of the many wounds, parents have to debride their children's skin before bandaging it, which is felt to be as painful as intentional torture.

There was no way whatsoever I could have been prepared or could have prepared myself for the prospect of parents being obliged daily to act towards their children in ways everyone knew was inflicting excruciating pain. Young children could not be expected to mediate such sensations into dignified suffering. The pain was just too painful to be distinguished as benevolence or care. I found myself just running out of empathy - if that is the capacity to step into another's shoes. This was truly outside of what I could conceive. Nor could I fathom what it might be like to revive a comatose child who was arresting and how such a hazard could ever become a part of my everyday life. I felt like an alien, and the very best I could hope for was a very rough translation, however uncertain and circumscribed by the limits of my own experience.

I had to ask myself - to what extent can a person participate in another's feelings or ideas? After all, empathy rides on the faith that the grounds of experience between myself and others are similar, such that I can know what another is feeling, based on what I might feel in such a situation. But what if the situation remains beyond your grasp, despite your best efforts to imagine yourself into it?

I decided to take ethnography (or, better put, the *doing* of ethnography) as my means of operating. Rather than thinking of myself as possessing some 'expert knowledge' that I might apply to those consulting me, I made seeking out fellow-feeling as my primary concern. After all, in every instance, the various expert knowledges had exhausted themselves of their very own expertness or frankly admitted that they could do no more than palliative care. For me to presume to substitute some sort of 'psychological' expert knowledge would have been insolent and immediately rendered me 'suspicious'. By the same token, my 'suspiciousness' could very well have been experienced as blaming, as had often been the case, despite my best efforts to redress that.

Other questions I was asking myself were:

- How could I request people in peril to stop seeking rescue but rather turn to themselves and each other?

- How might I proffer something other than a 'miracle cure' to take the place of the forsaken 'medical cure'?

- How could we all take up different relationships with each other and the problem of suffering?

I had observed that the discourses of biomedicine and the discourses of miracles produce patients and petitioners who fervently looked beyond themselves for 'cure' and/or 'salvation'.

I chose to orient myself around the co-research metaphor both because of its beguiling familiarity and because it radically departed from conventional clinical practice. It brought together the very respectable notion of research with the rather odd idea of the co-production of knowledge by sufferers and therapist. What made this possible, in the first instance, was a fairly thorough-going externalising conversation, one in which the problem was a problem for everyone - and here I included myself. Here's where I parted company from the disinterested ethnographer. This has led, and continually leads, to practices to discover a 'knowing' in such a fashion that all parties to it could make good use of it. Such knowledges are fiercely and unashamedly pragmatic.

Ashley's story

Ashley was not yet three years old when his parents, Colin and Kathy, approached me about his severe dystrophic epidermolysis bullosa. They sought for me to prescribe his future and theirs, something I was quite unwilling to do. Instead we commenced to co-produce a sufferer's or insider's knowledge under the umbrella of reducing their suffering in general.

The Dystrophic Epidermolysis Bullosa Research Association became a precedent for what I have come to refer to as a 'community of concern'. I commenced advertising co-research practice in a very scrupulous and transparent fashion. It was advantageous, to be sure, that they themselves used 'research' in the very naming of their association. So difficult and rare were their circumstances that many swore they owed their very lives to the existence of their annual conventions and the forum of their quarterly magazine. With everyone's consent, I made it my practice to circulate the letters I wrote to one family around their community, thanks to their newsletter. At the annual convention, a day would be set aside for co-research. In the morning, I would review whatever co-research projects were underway (for example, the project Kathy and Colin and I had evolved, which I will show you immediately) with all their 'community' of around 200 people gathered around us. In the afternoon, groups would break into what they ironically called 'case conferences', made up of children, families, extended family, friends, and professionals to reflect on the 'knowledgeableness' of the family concerned. Such a knowledge would then be considerably enriched. Their own knowledges - often miles apart - were often evoked when referencing their own experiences with DEB against the co-researching agenda. Thrilling surprises were always in the air, which often set the co-research agenda for the next year. To bring this all down to earth, here is the first co-research letter circulated through the DEBRA Newsletter.

Dear Colin, Kathy and Ashley,

It was very pleasing meeting up with you and starting a conversation which I hope we will continue in the future. On my part, I am just getting to grips with DEB and the particular problems it presents to young people and their families.

First of all, I think it is important for me to set out my thoughts for your consideration. I am totally unconvinced that the answers you are seeking for Ashley exist within any professional knowledge. As far as I can see, medical knowledges don't apply themselves to the day-to-day problems confronted by Ashley, yourselves and your community. Many people seek that day-to-day knowledge from doctors and are sadly disappointed and at times angry. My position is very dissimilar. I propose that the knowledge, so particular to Ashley and yourselves, be developed by yourselves in co-research with me. That is, of course, if you wish my assistance. Co-research implies, firstly, that the answer is unknown but, secondly, that it can only be discovered by an experimental attitude on a day-to-day basis. Co-research is also based on the belief that parents and young people can find their own solutions to some of the effects of their medical problems, or at least reduce the effects of such problems in their lives and that of their families. An experimental attitude draws upon something parents already do, and that is the close observation of their children and their activities, noting small differences. This approach sponsors flexible solutions, ones that fit the particular developmental circumstances of young people and their families.

We discussed a number of points, some of which I thought might profit by further consideration, both by you and me. Kathy and Colin, you both would like to know conclusive answers to some very important questions regarding Ashley. I urged you against seeking this kind of information. Instead, I counselled you to raise a number of questions to your conscious awareness, all the better to experiment with. Instead of conclusions, I propose balance. I have found that those people who seek conclusions blind themselves to chance discoveries. They want the right answer when, in fact, there is no right answer.

What happens, then, is for parents to choose parent-supervision as the right answer, and if or when that doesn't work, to choose child-supervision in its place. All the time the search is for the right *answer. An experimental approach concerns itself with balance or, better yet, finding the balance between, say, parent-supervision and child-supervision (self-supervision). This allows for flexibility and new learnings. For example, in some circumstances, say learning a new skill, it would be more helpful to start out with 95% parent-supervision but then start tapering off so that by the time it becomes an old skill, the balance is now 95% Ashley supervising himself and his parents supervising him 5%. These balances will also reflect Ashley's age and stage and current levels of ability. So there is* no right answer; *there is only balancing, and that is an act that everyone can enter into.*

We talked in general about three basic dilemmas that need to be balanced if Ashley and his family are not to become unbalanced (and I have certainly seen that happen with young people who must struggle with chronic health problems):

1) Parent-supervision/child-supervision.

   The hazard of many young people and their families, as we discussed, is the tendency for parents to supervise their children well past the time when their children, if they did not have health problems, would be supervised. You must have seen many examples of parents of chronically ill children being vulnerable to over-supervision. Many of these children are particularly vulnerable to inviting their parents to over-supervise them at the same time as under-supervising themselves. This can lead to a 'disabling' vicious cycle, with parents supervising them more and their children supervising themselves less. The parents can forget to supervise their own lives and, as a result, they often become problem-centred and the family life (or what's left of it) revolves around the problem. The opposite or 'enabling' virtuous cycle sees parents inviting their children to supervise themselves more and, by doing so, they invite their parents to supervise them less. Now, Ashley is only 3, and in the above I am talking about children aged 1 to 17. Still, from speaking with you, I could see how you were giving Ashley some 'space' to supervise himself (and pay the consequences). Of course, your parent-supervision comes in, say if Ashley unwisely supervised himself and the consequences of his decisions were too harmful to him. Still, with DEB, I guess the only way to learn is the hard and painful way and the sooner he is able to decide wisely, the better. The above is merely a framework for a 3-year-old Ashley, remembering that the balance for a 4-year-old Ashley will be a bit different.

2) *Taking pressure off Ashley in regard to his problem/putting pressure on Ashley in regard to his problem.*

   Taking the pressure off and putting the pressure on is something of a restatement of the above. Once again, there is a problem of balance and the scales probably shift on a day-to-day basis, depending on Ashley's well-being. However, these terms allow you to revise matters on a day-to-day basis. For example, 'Ashley, today you suffered a fair bit, so we are going to take the pressure off you', 'Ashley, you had a good day today, so we are going to put some pressure on you, so we are going to expect you to clean up your toys', etc.

3) *Self-sensitivity/other-sensitivity.*

   Self-sensitivity and other-sensitivity: this is a critical issue for young people and their families. Having a chronic and painful health problem leads many young people to be exquisitely self-sensitive, as you might expect. It can also lead their parents to be very sensitive to them. This can lead, in turn, to a young person becoming very insensitive to others, particularly their parents, and many parents, especially mothers, becoming very insensitive to themselves. In the end, you have a young person who is self-sensitive/other-insensitive and parents, particularly mothers, who are child-sensitive and insensitive to themselves and their relationships. Once again, this is a question of balance, a balance that is constantly shifting. If you have kept this dilemma in mind, I can't believe you would allow matters to get out of balance much before you would make readjustments.

   I wonder what you think about the above and if you think this would be useful in providing a 'map' for deriving experiments, experiments that won't provide you with a once-and-for-all answer but rather day-by-day answers. I believe, too, that the more you apply these dilemmas, the easier it will be to

rebalance, should you consider it necessary. I'll stop here. Sorry for taking so long in getting back to you. I look forward to hearing from you and meeting up with you again. Feel free to send me any of your 'stories', which I hope in due course will be compiled by your Association and circulated from one family to another. These 'stories', when read together, will provide the reader with a sufferer's knowledge, a knowledge particular to the everyday life of a young person with DEB and their family. I look forward to assisting you, in any way I can, with this venture.
Best Wishes
David

The archives of the Anti-anorexia/Anti-bulimia League

Having considered the history of this co-research work, allow me to pass rather quickly to what I have been referring to for almost a decade as the archives of the Anti-anorexia/Anti-bulimia League. The problem of so-called anorexia/bulimia have consumed me up until recently. Anti-anorexia allows us, if we listen carefully, to hear what Anorexia has to say and how it says it. But it does not tell us its purposes or causes. That is for all of us to find out. How does anorexia enter a 'young woman's life, impersonate her for a period of time, before becoming her cruel ventriloquist? What is so frightening is that the words coming out of so many mouths in any number of mother-tongues are so much the same. For reasons such as these, should we then concern ourselves as to what is this 'power' that is pulling so many strings on so many lives? Furthermore, how does such 'power' spin so many deadly webs that entangle so many young lives, bleeding them of hope so that nothing but their annihilation is imaginable? How does anorexia conceal itself so that it can proceed without much resistance to speak of, or hardly any public outcry? Anorexia's 'power' is so treacherous, so insidious in fact, that it has young women torture and violate themselves while it remains in the shadows of their lives stalking them. Anorexia not only claims its innocence but goes further than this. It now promises these young women the means to escape the very web in which it has ensnared them. They are told that the strict adherence to anorexia's regimes of rules and regulations will 'set you free'. They are soon to learn that they can never satisfy anorexia and are now on a 'diet to death'. Each and very attempt to reach the anorexic standard, and their inevitable failure to do so, unwittingly tangles them more into the web. And the web now starts closing in on them, slowly but surely squeezing the life out of them.

It has always been my practice to heavily document it from my very early days as much for self-protection as anything else. Bob Dylan sang something to the effect that: 'If you are going to live outside the law, you had better know what the law is!' The philosopher Michel Foucault advised the documentation, authentication and circulation of 'alternative knowledges' if they were to do what he proposed was their work - that of critique. I have always kept this in mind. Anti-anorexic documentation has taken many forms, and the 'itineraries' of their circulation have become international, now being carried by fax and email. Perhaps the five boxes currently stored in my garage will soon move to some book, hypertext and/or electronic home.[2] To be sure, I'll still keep my boxes of archives as back-up.

Why did I choose the term 'archives' and come to think of myself as an archivist? First of all, an archive, according to the *Concise Oxford Dictionary*, 'is a place where public records are held'. In the early days, the archive operated in a very crude way - I would Xerox copies of archival material and post them on request. These archives have been both a resource to and exemplary tales of a 'counter-practice' - commonly known as anti-anorexia/ anti-bulimia - to what I refer to as the social practice of anorexia/bulimia.

Many have called upon these archival documents to inspire their own resistance. Often those who loaned the documents later wished to contribute their own. The most common response to being read a document has always been, 'Can I have a copy that?' This growing body of documents - these fragments of an 'alternative knowledge' - needed a name. *The Archives* was an obvious choice. Its main purpose was to merely store in good care and find ways to index it so anything could be easily retrieved. Many of the first generation of League membership bitterly complained that the various professional literatures concerning anorexia/bulimia either dismayed them or made them actively ill. The more autobiographical genre of the 'I am an anorexic' type seemed to offer readers little chance for escape. More than anything else, it remains a literature of despair.

I envision such an archive of resistance to be both a resource and a platform for anti-anorexic developments that are as yet currently unimaginable to me. I hope too that it will be the means to a movement that will operate both underground and above ground to conscientiously object to, resist and finally repudiate anorexia and bulimia.

I suppose by now 200 to 300 people from around the world have contributed to it, although not every document forwarded to me has been included. Most made their contribution for the express purpose of fostering disobedience and protest to anorexia. Many of the contributors suffered dearly for having done so by various forms of anorexic torment, but they did so nonetheless. Still, we should remember that. It is more than a decade old now, and sadly I have lost touch with some of its most notable contributors. But what wedded us all together into a 'community of concern' was this archival knowledge that provided a place to speak from and retreat to.

Such records of resistance tell too of the horrors and inhumanity of anorexia/bulimia, and lift those up who have suffered and are suffering so that we can witness their testimonies, keep their legacies alive and, most importantly, pay them our respects.

Speaking anti-anorexia - an anti-language

The documents within the archives can take many forms, as you will see, but what is common to them all is their *manner of speaking* - anti-anorexia - an anti-language, a radical form of an externalising conversation.

The following quotation is one of the first public statements by the so-called 'anorexic' Ellen West written prior to World War II. She was later to suicide. Or was she executed? But first let us listen carefully to her words, the only manner of speaking she had to express the horror of her life:

> *I don't understand myself at all. It is terrible not to understand yourself.*
> *I confront myself as a strange person. I am afraid of myself; I am afraid*
> *of the feelings to which I am defencelessly delivered over to every*
> *minute. This is the horrible part of my life; it is filled with dread.*
> *Existence is only torture ... life has become a prison camp ... I long to be*
> *violated ... and indeed I do violence to myself every hour of the day.*
> (Binswanger 1958)

If she could have spoken anti-anorexically, she might very well have proclaimed her conscientious objection to anorexia rather than such a confession of her supposed offences:

> *Anorexia, why are you trying to confound and confuse me so that the contradictions I experience as growing up as a woman in the Third Reich are obscured? Why did you appear just when I started to make myself up? How did you turn my critique into my estrangement? Why would you want to turn me against my very desires, wishes, opinions and appetites? And if I were to reflect with a community of like-minded women upon such matters as how and why you conscript us into prison camps where we are defenceless against your tortures and violations, might we turn against you rather than our bodies, minds and spirits?*

In my experience, once provided with the means to speak against anorexia/bulimia, almost to a person, everyone aged 12 years of age and over has railed against many of the 'psychological' and 'psychiatric' constructions of them as 'anorexics' or 'bulimics'. The 'stories' from the insiders are incomparable to the stories written about them by outsiders. Why is it that insiders regularly refer to anorexia as either a grotesque manifestation of evil or the devil, when such terms have otherwise been consigned to the dictionaries of the histories of words?

Documenting knowledge-in-the-making

What is most important to me about the archives is this: that the documents record knowledge-in-the-making and reveal it as such. There is no wish at all to use the conceit of 'completed knowledges' that promise to have all the answers. By comparison, the archive would wish to provide some of the best and most poignant questions and pertinent lines of inquiry. I am referring to the distinctive 'reading' the archives call for as *resonation*. The archives are read for inspiration rather than right answers, prescriptions, etc.

Here are some of my favourite questions to a person with whom I have just shared an archival document:

- *Lee, did Judy's account of her betrayal by anorexia ring any bells for you?*

- *Lee, did Judy's account of her betrayal by anorexia enable you to see anything about anorexia that it had been blinding you to up until then?*

- *Lee, did Judy's account excite your mind in any anti-anorexia way? And if so, how?*

- *Lee, were you able to connect in any way, shape or form with Judy's account?*

Since most documents are knowledge-in-the-making, most people resonate to this, although they may or may not concur with specific conclusions.

Robyn's unmasking of anorexia

One video document that has proved to resonate with many people's experiences has been Robyn's unmasking of anorexia.

David: Robyn, from what you have been telling me, does that mean you have unmasked Anorexia?

Robyn: Yes I have. In fact, unmasking Anorexia is crucial. It is the crux of the matter.

David: Can you tell me how you registered Anorexia unmasked for the first time?

Robyn: I had a fight with my parents. Fights usually herald several pro-anorexic days because, straight after a fight, I can't eat. It's like a button being pushed. I was tremendously upset and decided to hide down by the pool in the back yard. I then saw this ugliness that scared me witless but, at the same time, I was able to face it. I really identified it as an evil spirit. I felt its grip ... its bite. We were locked in combat for between a quarter and half an hour. It started with panic and guilt over what I had eaten over the day. Physically, I was feeling sick. I felt a gut dread ... an unfocused dread. But then for the first time, I saw its true face. I had never seen anything so hideous. It's a monster, black, with indistinct features. It was more an emotional concept. MY TORTURER. It did manifest itself as a force of being, an evil power. I got the feeling I could oppose it. I struggled with it in hand-to-hand combat. I prayed to strengthen my resolve. I won that fight but it wasn't a fight that was all mine.

Robyn then paused for several moments and, becoming far more relaxed and even serene, she proceeded with a kind of summary:

I've seen it now. It will never come to this again. I've seen its chilling side ... its cunning side. THE UNMASKING OF ANOREXIA is crucial. I think I know what it is now. Now when it tries to trick me, more and more I see them as tricks. It all began when I was 16, when I started blossoming as a person and had just started flowering. Anorexia takes away your ability to govern your own life and make your own decisions, and replaces this with a crutch, a false refuge, somewhere to run away to. Anorexia separated me from my hopes and dreams. It made me passive and out of the world. It disconnected my logic and my heart. It was as if my life was happening to me and I had no say.

Carla's story

Sometime after the making of this video with Robyn, I was to meet Paula Parsonage, a counsellor working for Community Alcohol and Drugs Service (CADS), through a decidedly strange set of circumstances. I was contacted by Kathy Menzies, the Director of CADS, asking if I would provide six sessions of counselling for Paula. This was the agency's protocol for any counsellor 'losing' a client. 'Why me?' I asked. I obviously misheard as I thought Paula's client had died of anorexia. I asked if I might contact Paula myself, firstly to give her my condolences, as well as make a time to meet. Kathy said that would be unwise as Carla hadn't died yet; rather she had recently been declared 'terminal' at a meeting Paula attended, along with Carla's family and all professionals associated with Carla's care. Paula, quite extraordinarily, refused to withdraw her services, although all other professionals agreed to do so. I immediately asked Kathy if she would be willing for me to use the 'posthumous sessions pre-humously'. Kathy laughed, thought for a moment, and agreed to this.

Paula, Carla and I met soon after. Carla was 38 and had had, according to her, 55 hospital admissions over the past 23 years ever since anorexia took over her life after she was sexually assaulted. She lamented how she had always, for as long as she could remember, wanted to be a nun and live a religious life. However, since this offence, anorexia had, in a manner of speaking, excommunicated her, forbidding her to enter a church, pray in private or even hang her cherished pictures of 'Our Lady' and 'The Bleeding Heart'. I surmised that over the course of so many hospital admissions, she would have had her fill of being asked questions. She heartily agreed, but probably was left wondering how we would fill our time. I proposed that we consult the archives and that I would read from them. Included in my readings was Robyn's unmasking of anorexia.

The following letter details our next meeting.

14.5.93

Dear Carla and Paula,

Carla, Paula and I certainly felt a long way behind you in terms of your anti-anorexia. And I was touched to learn that all the laughs we shared in our first meeting was the first time you had heard the sound of your own laughter in over 20 years. I wish I had been aware of that at the time so I could have relished each and every one of your laughs and jokes. Anorexia does require people to be deadly serious and, to be quite frank, I think it's deadly boring.

After our first meeting, you told us of the onset of some 'uncanny experiences, religious in nature', which provided you with an anti-anorexic vision. When we got thinking about it, your vision came to you something like the visions Robyn documented in the League archives.

Carla, why do anti-anorexic visions take such unusual avenues to bring new thoughts, ideas, etc. to your conscious mind?

Carla, do you think these visions were an expression of anti-anorexia bursting through the defences of anorexia and the spell it had cast over your life for the past twenty-three years of 'hellishness'?

What you told me about your vision was this: 'I've lived this long. There must be a purpose in it. I am a FIGHTER and have survived so many physical ailments'. And you suspected that it was your personal faith and spirituality that was at the bottom of this. You wondered if it might be Our Lady, and then

told us how anorexia had 'forced me to neglect her'. In your visionary experiences, you were able to see a future for yourself, even though it is as yet unclear.
Did anorexia tell you that you were unworthy of your faith?
Did anorexia try to strip you of your very soul?
Was a hint of the future refreshing to your soul? Did it hearten you in any way?

Through this visionary experience, you thought you now had embarked upon an anti-anorexic direction. To do so, you must have broken the spell of anorexia. Can you record for the archives your 'first steps', because the 'first steps' are always the biggest steps, even though they seem minuscule at the time?

On reflection, you thought the fact that 'I didn't believe in myself' may have advantaged anorexia in deceiving you into believing in its promises of salvation. And you wondered, too, if 'I hadn't been searching in the wrong direction. I was hoping for something to drop out of the sky'. When did you realise that anti-anorexia could only be gained by resistance and struggle? How did that dawn on you? In fact, you said of late, 'I am getting more positive and starting to believe in myself'. And this is in the face of anorexia's attempt to isolate you and drive you to self-execution, one way or another. For example, anorexia has got you out of practising the art of conversation and tried to convince you that you were nothing but an 'anorexic' and that there was nothing left of you as a person.

In your visionary experience, you turned against perfection too. It provided you with a rallying cry: 'NOBODY IS PERFECT!'

And it made you fully aware of the trap anorexia had ambushed you into: 'The more you try to be perfect, the more inferior you feel. The more people blame you for anorexia, the more you feel like a second-class citizen. And then you start to feel that anorexia and its torture, punishments and enslavement is what you deserve because you are no longer normal.'

Both Paula and I witnessed a lot of your self-confidence shining forth. This is what you had to say: 'I am working on getting some sort of control over my life'. This didn't satisfy my curiosity and I asked more questions of you. You replied: 'My faith is mine again. All this is happening for some reason. There is some power behind all this.' Well, I was convinced of your power, although that is not to take away from the power of anorexia. As you told us, you had previously thought that if you just went along with anorexia's demands and requirements of you, you would finally satisfy it and it would leave you alone. You then found out to your dismay that it would not rest until it had you sign your own death certificate.

It was now you cried out those slogans to rally your spirits:

NOBODY IS PERFECT!
I'VE GIVEN UP TRYING TO PLEASE MEMBERS OF MY FAMILY
I'LL PLEASE MYSELF INSTEAD!
I'LL GO MY OWN WAY!

You went on to tell us that 'I used to feel guilty if I ever did anything for myself to make myself feel good', but that now 'I feel that I have come out of a dark hole ... out of a nightmare'.

Anorexia is a formidable enemy, but anti-anorexia is just, is it not? And I believe justice should now be on your side. And in addition, is there some divine presence behind what you refer to as those 'uncanny things'? What do you think of the fact that you can now 'pray well' again after all these years? And that you stumbled over the Old Testament verse of 'a time for everything - a time for war and a time for peace'?

Carla, I submit this question to you with the utmost sincerity. Is it your time for an anti-anorexic crusade? Has peace and submission to anorexia brought you anything but your near-annihilation? Is your anti-anorexia your holy cause? When I asked if anorexia had ever taken your soul, you fervently denied this and reassured me that that had never been contaminated by anorexia.

Yours anti-anorexically
David

What the League has meant to me

I would also like to tell you what the League has meant to me. For me, this work has been extraordinarily difficult on so many fronts. How many limbs have these families and I gone out on, that if one broke, death would have been very likely. I cannot tell you how often in the solitariness of my office, I too would appeal to the League, embodied in its archives. I have lived for several years now with the comfort that Lee, Sarah, Brett, Bryce, Paula, Fran, Eva, Gloria, Jenny, Jo-anne and so many more are both behind me and beside me. Anti-anorexia has become my place too to stand and speak from, for at times you can feel invisible - even though you're not - but this is certainly worth entertaining when you work against evil.

The Leagues as 'friends-in-arms'

To end, let me tell one final story. Mary, aged 17, had pulled herself out of the quicksand of anorexia in 1997 and 1998 for the time being. It was painstaking for her parents, Warren and Sharon, and myself. However, when she was faced with her final secondary school examinations late last year, we all feared that every freedom she had reclaimed had been forfeited and she would perish. Warren, usually a strong contributor to any anti-anorexic matter at all, sat with his head bowed, tears running down his cheeks and pooling onto his shirt collar. Sharon, also a strong and thoughtful commentator, seemed frozen into stillness and glacial silence. It seemed as if Mary had come to say farewell. I found this unbearable and wrote to her from the very 'heart' of the archives.

Dear Mary,

I wanted to write you after our meeting on Thursday. I strongly felt Anorexia, once again, pulling you away from us and down, insinuating that there was no other 'world' for you other than his Hell, where you might sit beside him as his Queen. It was unnerving for me, and, judging by Warren's helpless tears of frustration, it is for us all. Before I had time to put my fingers to my typewriter, your mother rang to reassure me that you were able to come back to us a bit. That was a great relief to me, and I know it was to Sharon and Warren. However, it did delay my response.

Mary, I am writing to you in defiance of Anorexia and all that it stands for. I swear to you - and all those murdered by Anorexia are my witnesses - that nothing will prevent the League from keeping a 'place' open for you - a place to stand and take a stand for your life and entitlements to happiness, peace and fulfilment. Admittedly, such a Resistance must at times go into hiding underground and at other times strike fiercely. And we do sustain losses. But such losses are trivial compared to those suffered at Anorexia's hands. After all, it will even 'eat your smile for dessert'. What kind of life is it that Anorexia promises? To be a well-dressed Barbie-puppet, looking pretty? What do you make of her smiling as she goes about measuring herself up to perfection and torture?

What does Anti-Anorexia promise? Nothing but a place to stand and hold up a mirror for you to see Anorexia without its mask of benevolent solicitude. It is a longstanding tradition in the annals of punishment and torture that the executioner always keeps his face well hidden, is it not? From an anti-anorexic standpoint, Anorexia can no longer blindfold you or keep you in the dark. Now can you see what there is to see? Can you speak out against Anorexia because you have the language to do so? Can Anorexia conceal its intentions for you any longer? Are its promises turning to dusty betrayals?

If my experience in the League over the past 10 years is anything to go by, there will be struggle, but I suspect in and out of those very struggles, you will forge yourself for yourself. I can assure you there will be fun and celebration along the way. And one day you will decide for yourself to put your arms down. However, will you ever set your vigilance aside? After all, Anorexia is nowhere and everywhere: Anti-anorexia is merely somewhere.

Mary, we remain your sisters, your brothers, your comrades, and your friends-in-arms. We remain where we are, even if sometimes we must go underground, but we will never surrender. If I am any judge of Sharon and Warren, I believe that they would never surrender either. Never!!! To be one of us, there is no measurement, no examination and no assessment. Your suffering, which is so evident to all of us, is your welcome.

Welcome back even if you have to jump the hurdle of your 'examination'. We want you to know we abhor examinations. You are more than enough for Anti-anorexia!

I look forward to catching up with you next week.

David, on behalf of The Anti-Anorexia/Anti-Bulimia Leagues

Notes

1. David can be contacted c/- The Family Therapy Centre, 1 Garnet Rd, Westmere, Auckland, New Zealand.

2. By the 1990s, the requests for archival material had became too onerous and the means of its distribution too unwieldy and expensive. The archives themselves were growing at such a rate that they were starting to defy my means to even store them. From 1992 on, many League members had been urging me to compile the archives and make them available by way of a book. As such, this would have required the format of an encyclopaedia and I doubt if any publisher would have considered that a viable proposal. I could not imagine my way out of this, until I hit upon the idea of a conventional book (well, not really that conventional) that could be read for itself at the same time as serving as an orientation for a more complete archive, lodged on a website. Hypertext space is far more generous and less costly than textual (book) space. Otherwise, I should have been required to reduce, say, 5,000 pages down to 200 pages and, no matter how hard I tried, it was an utter impossibility. The integrity of the archives had to be maintained at all costs rather than an 'anti-anorexic' book of greatest hits. A manuscript is currently being prepared by Rick Maisel (Berkeley), myself and Alisa Borden (Los Angeles) for W.W. Norton, and is tentatively titled 'Anti-anorexia/anti-bulimia: Archives of Resistance'.

References

Binswanger, L. 1958: 'The case of Ellen West.' In May, R., Angel, D. & Ellenberger, H.F. (eds), *Existence*. New York: Basic Books.

Wynne, L.C., Shields, C.G. & Sirkin, M. 1992: 'Illness, family theory and family therapy: Conceptual issues.' *Family Process*, 31(1).

17.

An HIV story:
Secrets and surprises

by
Paul Browde [1]

Gugu Dlamini, a volunteer working to persuade South Africans not to discriminate against HIV infected people, was beaten to death last November by her neighbours. They accused her of bringing shame to her community by revealing that she was HIV positive.

I too was born in South Africa, and am living with HIV. I recognise my privilege in being free to write this story. Gugu Dlamini's voice was silenced, mine is not. I dedicate this paper to her.

I recently returned from the narrative therapy conference in Adelaide, where I presented a workshop that came out of conversations I have had with my friend and colleague, Murray Nossel. Murray could not be in Adelaide, so he appeared in the workshop through video-taped conversations.

The workshop involved the performance of a dialogue we have been engaged in for the past ten years, in which we explore the effects that HIV has had on our community.

I went into the conference wondering whether what I had to say was relevant or appropriate to speak about. As a professional and a therapist, there is a lot of evidence in my world that my personal story should be kept personal, and that there is no place for it at a conference of my peers. I wondered if I was doing this for some kind of personal gratification, and to some extent whether that meant there was something wrong with me.

The reflections from the audience greatly enlarged the description I have of myself. I have returned from the conference with knowledge of the impact of this story, the effect that it has on people. I understood, on a visceral level, that to include living with HIV as part of the identity I choose to present to people is a powerfully political act.

Through the reflections of people at the conference, I came home from Australia with a richer understanding of what it means to me to be living with HIV. It is a complex multi-dimensional experience, that goes way beyond being a long-term survivor.

Murray and I have been invited to Adelaide next year, to continue the conversation at the conference, as one of the keynote addresses.

This paper consists of some of the stories of my own experience, that provide the context to our dialogue. Some names have been changed to protect confidentiality.

San Francisco - December 1984

It was in San Francisco in December 1984 that I met Larry. He was a social worker in ward 86, the AIDS ward at San Francisco General Hospital. I was a medical student doing an elective in Psychiatry up the hill on Parnassus. I was very interested in seeing what Larry did at work. One Thursday I joined him for the day. It was interesting and also shockingly sad. Young men were hooked up to intravenous drip bags in the waiting room, watching re-runs of 'I Love Lucy', chatting and laughing. These patients seemed used to their illness, they related to one another with humour and familiarity. All of them were young men with AIDS. Some were covered with the red spots of Kaposi sarcoma and all were very thin. Larry introduced me to the doctor in charge of the ward. One of the nurses showed me the whole set-up. I remember wishing that I worked in such a place, so gay-friendly, a place where I saw people felt they belonged. Larry did great work, helping these men with services and counselling them.

Larry invited me to a party the following Saturday night. It was a birthday party of his upstairs neighbour, a well-known theatre person, in a very fancy area of San Francisco.

Saturday evening, I took time to get ready, dressing carefully, making sure I was well-showered and shaved. I dotted a little cologne on strategic points all over my body, including the little groove above my top lip, so that I could smell it. I entered the party a little daunted by the formality of it all, the tuxedos, the well-built, elegant men in white suits who harmonised with the women in black evening dresses, as they milled around the white baby-grand piano. I chatted with a few people, and was of interest to some. I was an exotic foreigner, twenty-three years old, a medical student and a South African. I was tall, had dark curly hair, black eyes with very thick jet-black eyebrows and a persistent smile. I met Veronica, who was a friend of Larry's. She was a tall, handsome woman, with a Grecian nose. She was also a social worker and was off to spend time volunteering somewhere in South America. She and I connected. We had met earlier that week at the clinic, and we both knew Larry. We knew that one of us was going to go home with him that night, and we laughed at not knowing which of us it would be.

Larry arrived late. He was a slight man of average height. He had wavy brown hair, a narrow moustache, and a very childlike and open face. He was dressed in a checked flannel shirt, with denim jeans and seemed preoccupied and not particularly friendly. I was disappointed. I spent most of the evening chatting to Veronica, eating snacks, and listening to the classical pianist, who entertained to much applause. It was getting late, and Veronica was leaving. I decided to leave with her. We exchanged telephone numbers and agreed to meet for lunch later that week. After saying our good-byes, we walked down the white staircase to the street, Larry followed us. Larry was obviously in a quandary about who to invite home with him. He had slept with Veronica the week before, I knew - she had told me. I kissed Veronica goodnight, and clumsily hugged Larry, as I left them, feeling lonely and deflated.

'Paul' - it was Larry calling out to me - 'Want to come in for a drink?'

I spun round with relief, and walked the few awkward steps towards Larry and Veronica, who now looked disappointed.

'I didn't know what to say to her, it was a little difficult, but I am so happy to have you in my home. Just relax, make yourself comfortable.'

By now we had entered his basement studio which was magically illuminated with tens of recently lit candles. It cast a gentle light on his small apartment, the corner of which housed the bed, on which there was a large, inviting, white down comforter. He must have sneaked out of the party to prepare the room. There was tranquil music playing, creating a peaceful and romantic atmosphere, and Larry was charming, and beguiling. We had a passionate evening. The next day, I was in love. I knew where I could bump into Larry and orchestrated doing so. The moment I saw him, it was clear that he was no longer interested. He was aloof and cold, and I was miserable and lonely.

As we had arranged at the party, the next day I met Veronica for lunch, hoping to commiserate. She told me over lunch that Larry was in a bad way, that the previous week he had found out that his T-cell helper-suppressor ratio was inverted. She told me that this meant that his immune system was damaged, that he was infected with the HTLV3 virus.

How could he be infected? I was baffled. He is a social worker, he would have told me, surely? Why had Veronica not warned me at the party? If she had told me, would I not have gone with him?

I had had unsafe sex with a man who was infected with HIV. What was going on in my mind? What was going to happen, and what was I to do?

Johannesburg, January 1985

I had noticed lumps behind my head. I felt them on the bony prominence behind my ear. I used to try and massage them away, to press them flat against my skull. Soon there were more lumps, in my groin, under my arms, behind my elbows. I was in my final year of medical school, and, try as I might to ignore them, after a while I had to take notice of them. My mother, an oncologist, was nonchalant about it. 'It's probably not serious, let's put you on antibiotics and we'll see in six weeks.'

Six weeks later there had been no change. 'Why don't we call Ronny and ask him to biopsy one of them?' my mother suggested. Ronny was my friend Susan's father and a well known surgeon.

Susan and I had met in bed some years before. One late night, at the end of a party, needing a place to crash, there had been only one double bed for us to share. We both lay there frozen, thinking the other was waiting for us to make the first move. Slowly and carefully, I am not sure how we got there, we began to talk.

'Have you ever wondered what it would be like to be sexual with someone of the same sex?' one of us asked.

'I have thought about it? How about you?'

'I have wondered. Do you think you would do it?'

'Maybe ... You?'

'Maybe ... Have you ever done it?'

'Sort of.'

'How often do you think about it?'

'Occasionally. You?'

'More than that.'

'Me too.'

'Really?'

'Yeah. Often actually.'

'Me too.'

'Really? That's amazing. Isn't it?'

'It is … Actually I think about it all the time.'

'So do I.'

'You promise not to tell anyone, and I can't believe I am saying this, but I think, maybe, I might be gay.'

'Hmm, I think maybe me too.'

Susan and I became inseparable. We shared our hopes and fantasies with each other. We spent our Saturday nights on the staircase of the gay club - Mandy's - both of us afraid and awkward, scared to talk to anyone else. We had each other, but knew that we would go our separate ways when I found my 'Dagwood', and she her 'Blondie'. When we were sufficiently depressed, we would leave Mandy's and drive around Johannesburg till dawn. Many a night we sat at 'The Dolls' House', where the waiter brought the tray to the car and clipped it onto the half-rolled-down window. 'Two toasted chicken mayonnaises and two chocolate double thicks please.'

Sometimes we would drive out to the airport and watch the planes taking off. The exotic foreign planes, escaping this small stifling world for lands of freedom and promise, like England or Australia. I spent a lot of time in Susan's house. My parents knew and respected her father, Ronny. He was a colleague of my mother's and a family friend. Susan's parents and my parents invited each other to dinner parties from time to time.

So it was that I took my lumps to Ronny's office, where he recommended that I have the lymph node in my left armpit removed and biopsied. Within days, a nurse was shaving my armpit smooth, and I was lying on the table, with my hand behind my head, Ronny's warm eyes smiling above his green mask as he swabbed me with cold iodine. 'Count backwards from 10 to 1.' I woke up with stitches and a short stabbing pain under my left arm, that I can still feel when I am tired or stressed.

Five days later my mother got the results of the biopsy: 'non-specific inflammation'. She was elated. 'I can tell you now. I have been so worried - you know me - I thought it was lymphoma.'

My family celebrated. My father popped champagne and toasted me: 'To good health, this is marvellous'. They all laughed with relief.

I, on the other hand, did not feel relief. I knew. I knew that this was not the end. It was a vague, inchoate knowing. It was an unconscious horrified knowing, a dread, that I couldn't even speak to myself.

Some days later, Ronny called me. He asked me to come and see him in his house, which I knew so well. I drove, more slowly than usual up the winding road to his house. I walked into his study, once Susan's bedroom I had known so well, and now, as if for the first time, I noticed the bookshelves, the desk, the leather chairs. I noticed the papers in neat piles on the desk. It was early evening and the desk lamp was lit, casting a large shadow of Ronny who sat across from me onto the beige curtains behind him. Ronny's eyes were still friendly, but his face looked different. I was aware of his glasses perched on the bridge of his nose, his grey curls and his large white teeth which seemed to grow as they began to move up and down, in unison with his deep voice. He had begun to speak. 'Paul, it is no secret that you are gay, everybody knows that.'

I was silent.

'So when you had the lymphadenopathy, I decided to test you for HTLV3 [as HIV was known in those days], and, I have to tell you, the results have come back positive.'

At that moment, time began to play with me. The space between his revelation and my response remains the longest moment I have ever lived. As if in a trance, I experienced my life, and encountered my own death. As with a dream, the specific smells, tastes, sensations, feelings, thoughts, desires, visions, sights and sounds elude me now. I know I saw a balcony in an ancient European city: a cocktail party, elegantly dressed people I had not yet met, bathed in yellow light, sipping wine, talking in muted tones, laughing earnestly.

I knew in that moment that my life had changed irrevocably, profoundly and forever. I felt my voice rising, from my belly, up into my throat and out into the air which had become viscous, thick, holding the sound like smog, it echoed.

'I wish you hadn't done that.'

'I didn't know whether to tell you or not. It has been a very difficult decision. I spoke to your GP, and we have agonised about whether or not to tell you. He even called the Lubavitcher Rebbe in New York, and he thought we should tell you. We all agree that I must tell you. I mean you must know - you never know you might want to become a surgeon.'

The next few days were very slow. Nobody knew much about this condition. I consulted with a leprosy specialist, who advised me to tell my mother the news. 'Look', he said, 'while we do our best to keep confidentiality, you never know. Your mother works in this system, and better she should find out from you, than through the grapevine.'

I was sent to Dr B, a renowned and feared chemotherapist. He was an imperious man, who never looked me in the eye, but stared at his desk with no expression on his face as he listened to my story.

'Well, we need to do a battery of tests. You should have a whole lot of blood work done, and you need a bone marrow biopsy. Go into the next room and get undressed. I will do the bone marrow now.'

'Now?' I was terrified. I was well. I didn't feel sick. I had not prepared for this. I was not ready for this sudden assault on my body, being pricked and prodded everywhere. Dr B continued speaking to his desk: 'It has to be done, we may as well get it over with'.

Within minutes he had pierced my hip with a wide bored needle, plunging it deep into my bone marrow. 'You will feel some pressure as I pull back on the syringe', he warned me. Pressure was right. He failed to mention excruciating pain, which, like the armpit pain, I can still conjure up during times of stress. I never got the results of the bone marrow biopsy, which I presume were negative. Nowadays we know that a bone marrow biopsy is unnecessary for the work-up of HIV infection.

It was around that time that my emotions switched themselves off. My life was bathed in a deadening numbness, which allowed me to complete my medical training. Troubled by the faint thought that I wasn't going to be around for very much longer, I decided shortly after completing my medical training to give up medicine completely and pursue my life-long dream of a career as an actor. I applied to a drama school in London, and was accepted to start the program the following August. All I needed was to live long enough to get there.

New York, May 1992

Not only did I live long enough to get to drama school, but I lived long enough to complete the training, and spend some gruelling months experiencing the life of an actor. After the humiliations of auditions, working as a gardener for $5 per hour, and much frustration, I realised that for me being an actor was in fact a dream. I decided to return to medicine, and chose to do my residency in psychiatry, a field which I thought was about talking to and listening to people. What could be better?

I interviewed for various residency programs. At one interview on hearing I was gay, the residency training director asked, 'Have you been HIV tested?' I replied that I had, and I lied that I was negative. 'Good', he said, 'Only because we have lost a couple of excellent residents to AIDS and it has been very hard on the program'.

I entered residency with my secret well-guarded. In my second year, I started medications. AZT made me extremely nauseous. My eyes felt hot, and I was always on the verge of vomiting, which I did a few times a day. I never told anyone at work, and managed to keep going to the hospital daily. It was during the time of my neuro-psychiatry rotation that I felt particularly bad. At the end of the rotation, the unit chief told me that he thought I was not doing as well as I should be. He thought that I lacked application and discipline. I never said a word. I would rather have been thought of as lazy than have risked telling the truth.

It was in my third year that I had my first experience of conducting individual psychotherapy. The young man I was therapist to was in his early twenties, and worked as a nurse in a nearby hospital.

One day, and out of nowhere he came into the session with the question, 'How are your T-cells?'

I was completely stunned, unable to think, consumed with fear. I said, 'What are you talking about?'

'Your T-cells. I know you are HIV positive, I saw it on the computer at the hospital.' The hospital where he worked was also the hospital where I received my care.

'That is not true', I answered, 'You must have the wrong person'.

'Isn't your middle name Eric?', he asked.

I was cornered. I didn't know what to do. I held onto my seat till the session was over, and then froze in a rush of terror. He knew this thing about me that no-one at work knew. I was going to lose everything. My job, my career, my future. They were all over.

I didn't know who to turn to. I had never told my supervisors. I discussed it with my friends at home, who were supportive, and shocked.

In my next supervision, I presented the situation to my analytic supervisor. I told him that the client had found out something about me that was extremely personal and that I didn't know what to do about it. My supervisor said that if there had been too much violation of the boundary I should terminate the treatment.

This was not an option. The young man had been coming back week after week asking me difficult questions. He asked me how it felt to know that he could ruin my career, or how it felt to know that I was going to die. I knew that stopping being his therapist was not going to leave me any safer.

I spoke to another supervisor. I decided to take the bold step of telling her the truth about what was going on. Her response was, 'Love him, just keep loving him'. Given the way I was feeling, this was easier said than done. I eventually found some help in the words of my own therapist, who invited me to look at the process of what was going on, rather than to focus on the content. I began to explore with the young man his aggressive feelings towards me, and my therapist's idea that he had a wish to destroy me. This was helpful within the context of an analytic style therapy. However, what was never addressed was the politics of secrecy, the fact that I belonged to a discriminated-against group. That I was forced to be silent, by the dominant forces for which the young man was merely a mouth-piece. It was a couple of months later that I realised that, until this was no longer a secret, I would never be free. I got together with a colleague whom I had met at an HIV-positive doctors support group, and together we designed a strategy. We applied to give a presentation about our experience at the annual conference of the American Psychiatric Association (APA). Once our proposal had been accepted, we went to the head of the department at our hospital, to our chairman, and to many of our supervisors, informing them of the paper we were to deliver. We told them that we would rather tell them in person than to let them hear about it through the grapevine.

Reactions were mixed. Some were muted 'thanks for letting me know'. Some supervisors were extremely emotional. One cried, and yelled at us, saying, 'How could you let that happen to yourselves?' We explained that it had been almost ten years for both of us. He was very surprised that people lived that long.

So I went to the conference and revealed my long-held secret to a room of about fifty colleagues. I told the story of the young man who had discovered the truth about me. I spoke of how I had heard doctors speak of people living with HIV, and of how it affected me when I heard such comments as 'He's a goner'. I spoke of the distress at hearing HIV positive people referred to on a ward round as 'SHPOSES' (which I was told stood for sub-human pieces of shit.) On expressing my distaste at that comment to the senior doctor who conducted the ward round, I was reassured that he was referring to people who had been infected via IV drug use, and not the gay community.

I spoke of how everything I had ever seen at the APA regarding HIV related to death, depression and dementia. I related to none of those categories. I spoke of how I had a happy life, and of how my partner and my families of origin and of choice were supportive and loving. Living with HIV had transformed my life and their lives, in many and varied ways, and I was tired of hearing the subject whispered about in the hallways.

I don't really remember the rest of that day. People came up to me, and congratulated me. Some people asked questions, and I imagine I answered them. However, my secret was no longer a secret. I was free to tell or not to tell, and no-one could ever use it against me again.

There are still circumstances in my life where people do not know. Some situations are still difficult for me. Is it necessary for me to tell every client who comes to see me? Whose need would that be fulfilling, mine or theirs? I still have some slight apprehension about certain people reading this article. For example, some of the elderly people I work with who may have a hard time coping with the fact that I am gay, not to mention the revelation about HIV. Yet, once again, writing this article, and publicly telling this story, is an act of liberation for me. I choose to write this piece, and to have it published. It is a political act, and I feel good about it.

As I said at the outset, at the next Narrative Therapy and Community Work Conference in Adelaide in February 2000, Murray Nossel and I will be conducting a workshop, and performing a dialogue exploring many questions this experience has raised. We will be performing a dialogue that asks many questions about HIV, and whose story it is. We look forward to seeing you there.

Note

1. Paul can be contacted c/- 700 West End Avenue #15D, New York NY 10025, USA, phone (1-212) 669 9008, email: poebe@banet.net

Reflections

18.

Reflections on language, power, culture and spirituality:
Our experiences of the conference

by

Raul Rojas, Pamela Montgomery
& Jesus Tovar[1]

Dulwich Centre Publications' first conference on narrative therapy and community work was full of colours and flavours. It was like a kaleidoscope rich in rituals and ceremonies that invited participants from around the world to celebrate our common hope for a better society. Taking part in the conference as participants and presenters had a profound effect on all of us. We were moved by the opening and closing Indigenous Australian ceremonies, the music and rhythms of different cultures, the sharing between peoples of different nations. The outdoor setting continually reminded us of our connection to the earth. We appreciated the deep spirituality that arose from the heartfelt presentations and conversations, from revered traditions so generously shared, and from the overall dedication to promote well-being at the conference and beyond.

We had the wonderful opportunity to participate in gatherings and group reflections with Indigenous Australians. These group experiences offered us insight and inspiration. We were able to share our joys and struggles in working with our respective communities. We talked about the challenge of reclaiming cultural traditions that could serve as sources of healing within the context of the dominant culture. Throughout our conversations, it was interesting to see similarities not only in the problems we face as marginalised cultures, but also in our conceptualisation of culture and spirituality as powerful instruments of transformation.

Reflections about language and power

The conference gave us the opportunity to participate in multiple accounts of people's lives. Since the structure of the conference promoted dialogue among all people attending, we didn't feel a separation between 'presenters' and 'participants'. We enjoyed the inclusive conversations that took place both in and out of the tents, during and after the presentations. A fascinating collective sharing ensued that revealed different ways of expressing common struggles and life experiences. Conversations were rich and varied, moving back and forth from the simple and concrete to the more complex and abstract as they wove the textures of people's lives. These dynamics inspired us to ask some questions:

- *What is it that allows people from different countries and cultures to share together common experiences?*
- *What are the old and new practices of language that come to inform the ways in which our lives are storied?*
- *How can theoretical frames honour complexity and at the same time be accessible to people and communities?*
- *How might the use of abstract occidental language to describe stories of people's experience create separation among persons and unequal repartition of power? How can this be prevented?*
- *Since conferences represent a collective practice of externalisation and validation, how can we use them in ways that allow for equal expression of voices from different groups and communication styles?*

These questions help us continue our reflections about language and power, about equality and diversity. We discuss them among ourselves and welcome conversations with others on these themes. Our hope is to continue developing both old and new practices that help individuals and communities move from limiting dominant descriptions to richer, more empowering life stories. We believe that richer descriptions aren't necessarily more complex ones. A fundamental value of old or new descriptions is to bring clarity, peace, and self-determination to people's lives. A sense of empowerment can stem from language that reflects concrete realities and makes sense to each community. And there exists also a world of non-verbal communication. There is something beyond words that blossoms when people join to tell stories of suffering and hope, life and death, differences and commonalities. There is a dimension of connection and spiritual energy in which stories don't need to be expressed in words to be powerful and profound, a dimension in which dancing, touching, smelling, painting, working, or simply being together are as important as liberating verbal accounts.

Spirituality and culture

The spiritual dimension of many of the workshops and presentations was salient for all of us. We were drawn into the telling of the history of the Bowraville Gathering during the presentation, *Healing in Unity*. The 'spiritual healing journey' described encouraged us to think about the concepts of healing and spirituality in relationship to our own community workshops. Some sessions we attended on violence in families and communities brought in ideas about the role of spiritual beliefs and practices in stopping violence and promoting respect. And even when the term 'spirituality' wasn't specifically used, we sensed something sacred about the way in which respect, caring, accountability, and responsibility were named and explained. Comments from participants in our own workshop about respectful family relationships led us to think and talk about the elements of our community work that bring in a spiritual dimension. Participants especially commented on the power of the indigenous ceremonies we use in our workshops, as well as the community altar which acts as a focal point of respect, commitment, and transformation. Several people mentioned that we could spend more time on the opening and closing ceremonies and on exploring with participants the role of such ceremonies in promoting desired change. These comments have encouraged us to think more about how to create energetic spaces for the exploration of violent and respectful practices, how to use circles of people in ways that connect them with each other, with their past, and with future commitments to end violence. We have reflected more about the sense of spirituality that seems to emerge from the various levels of connectedness and about how this spirituality can promote sharing and forward movement in respectful ways.

Inspiring influences from the conference

As we mentioned above, our conference experiences have led us to think about elements of our work (spiritual, cultural, language, etc.), develop them further, and engage in ongoing conversations with colleagues and community members. We have felt energised to continue our current projects on the prevention of family violence - men's groups (*De hombre a hombre*), women's groups, (*Grupos de Mujeres Fuertes y Responsables*), and mixed gender groups for community conversations. We have also been inspired to continue writing an article about spirituality and culture, a topic that has interested us since we began our work several years ago. Through our conversations and writings, we want to continue reflecting on topics of importance to us: ways of bringing voices of our ancestors to therapeutic and community settings; honouring our cultural practices and traditions; reclaiming our particular ways of celebrating life; integrating spiritual elements that foster human connection and transformation; facilitating multicultural gatherings on the prevention of family violence.

The conference has offered us ideas for new projects in the Latino community. We have started working with day-labourers at a local community-based workers' centre to create a video. This idea came out of one of Michael White's workshops in which he showed a video of Barbara Myerhoff's work in a Jewish senior centre in Southern California. The video explored the importance of rituals, ceremonies, and stories of survival as sources of strength and unity among senior citizens. It also provided them with a strong sense of connection with their cultural heritage. We are in the process of producing a similar video with workers at the centre. We hope that the video will be a vehicle for exploring the role of culture in generating connections among people with a common heritage and in promoting the development of liberating narratives. We also hope to study the meaning of telling and re-telling stories within a cultural and spiritual context.

Gathering energies for the year 2000

We were touched by the way in which people representing so many different groups could sit together and explore collectively such themes as violence, respect, spirituality, culture, family relationships, and community projects. The inclusive nature of the conference gave richness to the descriptions and accounts. It allowed for a sense of coming together in a common enterprise, with the desire to work together instead of engaging in tactics of blaming and separation. We hope this aspect of the conference will be expanded even more in the upcoming conference in February 2000. We believe it reflects a sincere desire to work in ways that will ultimately join rather than divide human beings. We want to honour the bringing together of persons of different genders, sexual orientations, cultures, generations, and spiritual beliefs in a setting where they can speak to the problems they face and generate solutions of respect and equity.

Note

1. Raul, Pamela and Jesus can be contacted c/- Multicultural Narrative Team, PO Box 2565, Saratoga, CA 95070-0565, USA, email: Gamba7@aol.com (Jesus); Pamela408@aol.com (Pamela); raul.rojas@worldnet.att.net (Raul).

19.

Reflections on a Jewish journey

by

Yishai Shalif [1]

In February 1999, the months of Shvat and Adar 5759 according to the Jewish calendar, I attended the Dulwich Centre Publications' inaugural narrative conference. This was a journey lasting three weeks in which, apart from the conference itself, I participated in three workshops and many varied gatherings. This journey to Australia was a multiple one for me. I can think of three different journeys interrelating one with another. The first, which was the reason for me going all the way to Adelaide, was a professional journey to Dulwich Centre. The second was a journey to the Jewish community of Adelaide which I needed in order to carry out my religious practices. The third was a journey of Jewish connections and identity. All three unexpectedly ascended to a spiritual experience.

Practices of connection and the Jewish community of Adelaide

When I first decided to go to Adelaide for the conference I thought Adelaide was a small city in the south of Australia which probably had no Jewish community and certainly no Orthodox one. Later, to my surprise, I found out on the internet that one million people live in the Adelaide area. Through a friend who had visited Adelaide the previous year, I got in contact with a few members of a small Orthodox Jewish community which practised wonderful hospitality. For example, one family knocked on my door just before the onset of the Sabbath bringing me a freshly baked banana cake. This kind of hospitality, which continued during my whole stay, moved me very much and made me feel at home. When I walked out of the synagogue my first Friday night, I felt all I needed to do to get home was to walk around the block, whereas in reality that block would have had to be thousands of miles long!

'Number our days': Tellings, re-tellings, community and identity

The first encounter I had with Dulwich Centre and Michael White probably encapsulates many of my experiences and learnings in Adelaide. By mistake I arrived a day before the workshop I was supposed to take part in started, and I was very disappointed. Cheryl White, noticing this, offered me the opportunity of attending Michael White's workshop that day. Little was I to know how important that day was to be for me. In many ways, which I'll expound later, this first experience was to act as a blueprint for the rest of my experiences in Adelaide. What should be the first part of Michael's workshop for which I had come from the State of the Jews to faraway Australia to attend? A video about Jews.

Michael was showing the Barbara Myerhoff video, 'Number Our Days', about her anthropological research with elderly Jewish people in Venice, California, in the 1970s. I think I cried almost throughout the video (approximately 25 minutes) and I wasn't the only one. Michael showed the video in the context of explaining that identity is formed socially, within performing practices of culture and tradition.

The culture of those elderly people who immigrated to the US from Eastern Europe was very familiar to me. One of the scenes showed an old lady who fed the pigeons daily. She was telling how she chased away dogs and young boys who wanted to disturb her. The conviction of her actions and her tone of voice and accent reminded me very much of my grandmother and my wife's grandmother, who both came from Eastern Europe and endured many difficult times with courage and dignity. The thin crooked legs of the old ladies which were photographed so artistically reminded me of my own grandmother's thin legs which carried her full figure for 82 years. The Kiddush, Kaddish, Chazanut (Jewish cantor singing) music and symbols all struck a chord in my internalised cultural background. All those aspects are very similar to the Jewish tradition I practise today.

I wasn't born a practising Jew. Only as a teenager did I decide to take upon myself to become an observant Jew and to practise Halacha (Jewish Law). One of the main motivations for my change was a historic perception of the need to continue the tradition that my ancestors cherished so much and for which they had sacrificed and suffered so much. I saw no meaning in living in a Jewish state without those practices. Seeing those elderly people living in old age those traditions in their day-to-day practices, and communicating by their actions how important they were for them, touched my innermost feelings, thoughts and dedications.

Tying all this into narrative therapy moved me and not only in the cultural context. It gave me new understandings of some of the reasons which so attracted me to narrative ways of working. I would like to mention a few points which were raised for me by that fabulous video:

1. As I mentioned before, Michael White showed the video to express the ways in which identity isn't created solely in the individual realm, rather in the social and communal arena.

2. This identity is very much affected by the tradition and culture in which a person has grown up.

3. Barbara Myerhoff stresses the importance of the particular practices of tradition and culture.

4. One of the central themes of the video is the fact that telling and re-tellings not only describe a past experience but are very much creative of new or transformed identities.

Listening, sacredness and 'judging your friend favourably'

I feel that the above understandings create the possibility for a kind of listening within which the stories of people acquire a sacredness. This reminds me very much of the Chasidic tradition in which stories are important. Within this tradition it is acknowledged that, upon deeper exploration, even the most unsacred actions with the stories of Jews acquire a sacred meaning and understanding.

Another aspect in this process of re-telling and valuing stories within Jewish tradition is the positive viewing of what could seem negative, bad or evil. This is an expression of a fundamental Jewish value called 'judging your friend favourably'. Some people may interpret this value as an act of righteousness, but if one studies the traditions seriously, I believe it is clear that this value has a constructive meaning. There is value in this favourable judging, not so much in relation to revealing the 'truth', but in creating understandings which have positive effects in the 'real' world.

It isn't hard to see that already, on the first day of my Australian experience, my professional journey and my Jewish journey were interweaving in a way which was spiritually valuable to me. All the above understandings have had a tremendous effect on my therapeutic practices, on the process of taking the therapy out of the therapy room and tying the real effects of the outside world to therapy.

Taking therapy out of the therapy room and bringing the outside world into therapy

If I could sum up in a few words the most important professional issues I learned in my three weeks in Adelaide, I'd mention two particular themes. The first being to take the therapy *out* of the therapy room and bring the outside world *into* the therapy room. The second, which evolves almost naturally out of the first, is that therapy isn't separate from the life of the therapist or the patient.

Almost all the workshops I attended during the three weeks related to taking the therapy *out* of the therapy room and bringing the outside world *into* the therapy room. It was, however, the people from The Family Centre of Lower Hutt, New Zealand (Kiwi Tamasese, Charles Waldegrave and Flora Tuhaka), who most challenged me in relation to breaking the barrier between the therapy room and the outside world. They presented a philosophy and a record of action which believes that dealing with social injustice within the therapy room without taking it into the social arena is a way of co-operating with that injustice. For that reason, they have taken part in many actions for correcting social injustice. They carry out different kinds of research in order to sway the opinions of the public and of those with the authority to make social policy decisions in New Zealand. Recently they played a part in organising a march from all parts of New Zealand onto the steps of Parliament House in order to effect a change in anti-social laws. They also try to bridge the therapy room with the community in the ways they run the centre (Tamasese & Waldegrave 1993).

A parallel tale

Just as I was thinking through the ways in which broader issues of injustice inform our work and lives, I met a person within Adelaide's Jewish community (I will call him Salomon here, although that is not his real name) whose personal story taught me a great deal. I received a warm invitation from Salomon to stay with his family and he was persistent in inviting me to have a meal with them. Even though they didn't run a Kosher home, they were prepared to go through any procedure (including using boiling water to make some of the utensils kosher) to enable me to eat with the family. I ended up visiting this family several times and sharing in some inspiring conversations which interrelated very much to the issues I was thinking through at the conference.

Salomon had a lot of questions relating to the issue of keeping in contact with people who in his eyes had committed unjust actions. As an answer to curious questions of mine as to where he acquired this sense of justice, Salomon told me a number of wonderful stories. His mother and father moved to Egypt from Turkey[2] and he grew up in a household together with his grandmother. His grandmother used to tell him a story of her father who was a man of average means belonging to the local Jewish synagogue. One time the rich members of the Synagogue decided that since the wooden benches were too hard they would buy cushions to sit on. Salomon's great-grandfather spoke out on behalf of the poor people and said one of two things should happen. Cushions should be acquired either for everyone or for no-one. Another story Salomon shared was about the attitude his grandmother had towards the family's Egyptian servant. Salomon said he always felt it was unfair that he went to a good school and their servant, who was just as intelligent, would never have a chance for any academic education. When I asked Salomon what could have evoked a sense of justice in his life, he told a story about his grandmother. Many times she told them to give blankets to the poor. She said they had plenty and there was no reason that the others shouldn't have the comfort too. This seemed to me a living example of what our sages say. Hearing these stories encouraged me to explore the ways in which our traditions, both within our families, and within our cultures, speak to us of working for social justice.

Salomon is not just an active member of the Jewish community who many times helps to be one of the Minyan (ten people needed for public prayer by Jewish Law), but he is also a member of the Chevra Kadisha (which literally means the holy group and practically means the group of people which takes care of burying the dead). The work of the Chevra Kadisha is done without any compensation. It moved me to be witness to how much of what seems a 'simple' Jewish life is full of so much dedication to justice and the practices of benevolence and kindness.

These stories seem to me to testify to a deep sense and tradition of social justice. They also assisted me in understanding how traditions of social justice are created and re-created through tellings and re-tellings of stories within a social and cultural context.

Becoming a Jewish priest

Unexpectedly, part of what I assumed to be solely a professional journey became a Jewish and spiritual journey too. During the first week I was in Adelaide, there were more than 100 people who were attending different pre-conference workshops. Each afternoon after the workshops, Dulwich Centre organised an informal gathering over a glass of wine. For me, these became quite remarkable get-togethers.

From the beginning, my external appearance which included a Kippa (skull cap) a Tzitzit (four sets of eight threads tied to a garment placed just under the shirt, with the threads dangling from the sides)[3] and a beard, made my religious Jewishness very apparent. Due to this, I found myself becoming what I called jokingly a 'priest' as different people 'confessed' their Jewish identity and stories to me.

One of the first people I was introduced to was Paul Browde from New York City. We had a short enjoyable conversation at the end of which Paul told me that he sees a lot of the 'black Jews' (the very orthodox Jews who wear black coats and hats) in New York City but that he had never spoken to one before. He felt that our conversation had the effect of breaking a barrier. I was to find later that these open conversations would break a lot of barriers, not the least of which were some inner barriers of my own.

The two voices: 'Judging' and 'Valuing'

Another conversation I shared was with Jan Cooper, in which we shared ideas about the ways in which narrative ideas and ways of working fit with our Jewish roots. I must stress that this experience took place even though we have very different ways of practising our Jewish identity. I stress this point to illustrate how I had to make an inner decision during the conference. One voice in me, which I can call the 'Judging' voice, competed with another which I found hard to name. A few names went through my mind, including 'listening', 'hearing stories', 'the sacredness of people's experiences', 'connecting'. These are probably all good names for this other voice, however, after writing and thinking about it, another has come to my mind - 'Valuing' which in some ways encapsulates what these other voice encourages.

The 'Judging' voice was telling me to judge the stories of other people. Somehow this voice sounds very familiar. This is the voice that says, 'Why didn't you do more about your heritage?', 'Did you have to wait to hear from other people about their heritage to remember yours?' etc. The 'Valuing' voice which prevailed said, 'How wonderful it is to be honoured by people who share with you meaningful, intense, brave and unique stories of their relationships with their tradition, identity and future'.

I'm so grateful for the decision to listen to the 'Valuing' voice. It felt like living what we learned. Through this process, re-telling became not only a concept but a reality in my/our identity. I felt the practices of listening and telling re-membered me with these specific people, the Jewish people and humanity as a whole.

Meeting and listening to stories of different cultures as awakening one's own heritage

Part of what allowed this personal development was the way the conference was structured. There was a lot of space in the conference and the workshops a week before and after for the voices of Indigenous peoples. They evoked a lot of emotionality from the participants and made a lot of people think of their heritage, traditions, and culture. Let me give just one example.

I took a workshop with The Family Centre from Aotearoa/New Zealand. They had three people giving the workshop: Kiwi (a woman belonging to the Samoan community in New Zealand), Flora (belonging to the Maori community), and Charles (a *pakeha*, which means a white person). The opening ceremony to the workshop was fascinating. They first opened in the native languages, then they sang in the native language and later they translated it. Part of what they were saying was a greeting and a blessing to all of us coming from the different islands of the world, the island of Australia, the island of America, the island of Africa, etc. They mentioned the people of Australia inviting us and they mentioned their ancestors that are blessing us together with them.

Later Kiwi came over to me and gave me a book to read, written by Albert Went (1991), a Samoan man who is a professor of English Literature in

New Zealand. I couldn't put the book down. It was about a Samoan woman who takes her 75 year-old father, who never left Samoa before, for a pilgrimage to Israel. Would it be possible to find two geographical spots that are further apart? Two cultures that are more different? And yet I came to Australia to see that there can be made connections and spiritual closeness even in what may seem so far apart.

The last Jewish lunch: re-telling and re-membering

Somehow the atmosphere surrounding the conference and pre-conference workshops stimulated the creation of many spaces for different cultural meetings. One of those spaces was the 'Jewish lunch' - an idea originated by Jan Cooper[4]. On the third and last day of the conference, those of Jewish background, and anyone else interested, were invited to eat lunch together in one of the tents. A few dozen came together and shared their stories. As Jerry Gale describes, this was a special gathering:

Normally I would be ambivalent about such a meeting, feeling guilty for not being a member of a Jewish temple or following a strong Jewish practice. This event was different for me. It involved different people sharing their stories of being Jewish, coming out as Jewish, being isolated/persecuted as being Jewish, and much more. It touched me in different ways, and in the closing, when Jan suggested we sing a Hebrew song, the song selected was a song that I have sung to myself (quietly) for many years for comfort. I was moved to tears to participate in the singing.

During the lunch I shared a story of my own. I wasn't born into a fully practising religious family. One of the things which drew me to become more observant was the historical aspect. What did our ancestors live, struggle and sacrifice for? Why is it worthwhile to live in Israel, with all its hardships and wars? My maternal grandmother came to what was Palestine after the First World War after going through pogroms in the Ukraine. Her father and some sisters remained there. After the fall of Communist USSR, her youngest sister came to Israel with her son. She told me that during the Second World War her father (my great grandfather) and his children escaped the Germans by fleeing to Asiatic USSR. In the midst of the fleeing, she gave birth to her son. In those days the communist rule forbade the Jewish circumcision and anyone who would dare transgress the law was in danger of being sent to Siberia. My great-grandfather, however, took the chance and circumcised his grandson on his own.

During the lunch gathering, there were many stories told about journeys of Jewish identity. Stories of hardships, of turmoil, and of resistance and pride. Stories so different from one another and yet we were together. At the end of the gathering, just as at the beginning, we placed our hands on the shoulders of the ones sitting close to us and sang together in Hebrew.

The effect of my re-telling on my own life

Somehow, the rumour of how important the Jewish gathering was for many of us spread around, and David Denborough asked me to be interviewed on narrative, Judaism and spirituality. I don't remember most of David's questions, but I still hold in my heart the special feeling I felt while answering them. I was using a language I had never used before. Even though I'm what is considered very religious, I have always refrained from using what I call 'holy' words – such as 'sacred', 'holy', 'divine', etc. I have always felt a sense of estrangement from the way these words are used. However, suddenly, in faraway Australia, I found myself feeling that only these words were fitting to describe appropriately what I felt about people and their stories. Witnessing people's stories is an experience which I feel it is only fitting to describe as spiritual. The kind of attitude expressed in such a word gives the notions of respect and empathy a new dimension. For some reason this has a liberating feeling to me. Maybe it is a sense of freedom from those modern discourses which make us step back from 'holy' words and attitudes, which consider such words and attitudes 'primitive'.

This experience felt somewhat similar to when I read something of the work of Melissa Griffith and James Griffith (1985, 1994) who speak about the ways in which modern professional discourses separate us from the rich and varied experiences that people have of God. Reading Melissa and James' work has enabled me to have some most interesting conversations with people about very meaningful aspects of their lives which are usually not spoken about in therapy.

The re-telling of the Adelaide experience in the interview, and now in this text, has had a tremendous effect on the way I conduct therapy, the way I practise the managerial responsibilities I have, and my many different interactions with different people. I find it easier to respect people's stories, to find the sacredness of people's narratives and to integrate better the work I do with my own traditions, culture, belief-systems and identity.

Farewell

At the end of the three-week period of the conference and workshops, the Dulwich Centre staff held a final small informal gathering. A song of farewell, using the same tune as the conference greeting song, was sung. A group of women from Mexico sang a song in Spanish and a few people from the group then asked me to sing a song in Hebrew. I chose to sing a song from the book of Isaiah (chapter 55 verse 12). The translation of the words is as follows:

> *As you leave in happiness*
> *and shall be escorted in peace,*
> *the mountains and hills*
> *will open their mouths in praise/song,*
> *and all the trees of the field*
> *will clap their hands.*

As I sang, I found it hard to stop the tears rolling down my cheeks.

Notes

1. Yishai can be contacted c/- 2/3 Mevo Livna, Jerusalem 97758, Israel, phone (972-2) 581 0173, e-mail <y_shalif@netvision.net.il>
2. Incidentally, his ancestors and those of his wife fought on opposing sides in the First World War. His ancestors were in the Turkish army and his wife's ancestors in the Anzac forces which fought together with the allied forces against the Germans and Turks.
3. This is one of the biblical commandments practised by religious Jews.
4. See Jan's article in this book.

References

Griffith, J.L. 1986: 'Employing the God-family relationship in therapy with religious families.' *Family Process*, 4:609-618.

Griffith, J.L. & Griffith M.E. 1994: *The Body Speaks: Therapeutic dialogues for mind-body problems.* New York: Basic Books.

Myerhoff, B. 1986: 'Life not death in Venice: Its second life' In Turner, V. & Bruner, E. (eds), *The Anthropology of Experience.* Chicago: University of Illinois Press.

Tamasese, K. & Waldegrave, C. 1993: 'Cultural & gender accountability in the "Just Therapy" approach.' *Journal of Feminist Family Therapy*, 5(2).

Wendt, A. 1991: *Ola.* Penguin.

20.

Wandering, arriving, and re-membering: Tales from the Jewish tent

by

Jan Cooper[1]

The diversity of the conference provided a backdrop for me to ask an important question: 'What if we provided a space for Jews to re-member themselves and to become visible within this community?' Over the years, I have become aware of the large number of Jews exploring narrative ways of working. I often wondered about possible links between Jewish culture and experience and the 'at-homeness' many Jews feel working within a narrative framework. I had begun to understand some congruencies and answers in my own life. For example, both share a worldview which values multiple perspectives on a 'living' narrative and text (Torah). Both encourage active curiosity, relational ethics and communal accountability.

And, at the cornerstone of each is the importance of social justice, contextualising people's difficulties in the fabric of society and doing one's part to improve the human condition. I was curious about having this conversation on a wider scale. During the conference, people from a wide array of other groups had begun to find one another - to share stories, their common struggles and make the invisible present and heard. I wanted to find members of my tribe to do the same.

In ancient times, Jews gathered in tents throughout their wanderings. When we gathered in the large tent in Adelaide, from a wide array of backgrounds and places, it seemed altogether fitting a tent would be our setting. Some came to the tent with easy enthusiasm. For others, it was strange, even painful, to find themselves there. Some shared a sense of relief in being able to share aspects of their lives within a Jewish context for the first time. We sat with only an hour to share together over lunch, knowing we could take days to listen, tell, and excavate our commonalities. There was at first some unease and unfamiliarity. What would be our territory with one another? Jews understand their lives through the stories of so many possible identities - religious, national, cultural, socio-political. Where to even begin?

After a blessing and a welcoming song in Hebrew, our tellings, laughter and tears began to slowly spill forth. Some told stories of connection and pride. Others spoke of disconnection and struggles with shame. Some could trace a clear lineage, while others only knew that a distant relative had been a Jew. There were Israelis present - both secular and religious. Some of us came from cities with large Jewish populations and some from places where Jews are such a minority there exists little opportunity to sit together. It felt very powerful to acknowledge ourselves to one another and to know that there were millions of stories to tell and waiting to be told. What was left unsaid was just as poignant. Once we became visible to one another, connections which might have been completely missed began to weave themselves across continents and histories.

What seemed most important was the permission to place any story of importance into a context of Jewish experience. The stories of these identities are rich and complex, speaking to the domains of family, religion, ethnicity, culture, politics, nationhood, values, spirituality, consciousness - a clear case of 'thick description'. There are, however, significant hurdles in the way of open expression and meaning-making among us. One of the legacies of anti-semitism, both past and present, is that of being relegated to inferior, outsider status. Not only do we experience this as a form of societal oppression in many of the countries we represented, but versions of this also operate internally. Some of us carry stories for example, of not feeling 'Jewish enough', or not knowing enough, or not being accepted by other Jews for different choices.

This is particularly true for people in the Diaspora who were born into Jewish families but have been dispossessed of Jewish community or have chosen not to connect with certain aspects of their Jewish identity. Because of this, it was my hope and belief that literally any story might be told as a Jewish one, if so desired by the teller.

Upon reflection, what seems most striking is that this rich hour of conversation and connection might have easily escaped us. In fact, my Israeli colleagues and myself (I am from the US) went back and forth the week before the conference about whether to go through with it at all. We later recognised that our hesitancy and doubt spoke to why it was so important to push on with the invitation and create a presence for ourselves and others. One of the concrete ways the problem of anti-semitism continues to operate is that the very challenge of showing up and being visible remains. Ask us to be visible as Jews, and even the most confident among us can experience some hesitation or fear. Going ahead with the meeting helped us to deconstruct this as a hallmark of the problem itself. What helped propel us further was the encouragement and enthusiasm of non-Jews who understood how critical this meeting could be.

Several non-Jews volunteered to participate as caring listeners. I will never forget Kiwi Tamasese of the Just Therapy team, giving me a big hug and proclaiming that she would gladly run around and locate all the Jews at the conference who would want to attend and usher them there herself!

Just prior to our meeting in the same tent, I attended the presentation by members of the Bowraville Aboriginal community.* As I listened to the accounts of the murders of their children and the hollow response from the larger society, I thought of the children who had been murdered in the Holocaust. I wondered how our re-tellings as Jews, which were to follow, might be a way to honour their memory through naming ourselves and becoming known to one another. As I departed from the tent, I imagined the children who had perished in both communities, smiling at us for having travelled such a distance from so many lands and viewpoints, to find one another in this place.

Note

1. Jan can be contacted c/- Center for Collaborative Change, 3300 E. 1ˢᵗ Ave, Suite 550, Denver CO 88206, USA, email: jtcooper@collaborate.org, website: http://www.collaborate.org

*   Publisher's Note

This presentation involved reflections on a gathering which occurred in the Bowraville Aboriginal Community in New South Wales, in September 1998. This 'Healing in Unity' project will be published later in 1999. If you are interested in obtaining a copy, please write to Dulwich Centre Publications.

21.

Music:
Voices of hope and survival

reflections by

Gloria Marsay[1] & Paul Browde[2]

on the workshop of the same name which was facilitated by
Busi Nthoba & Lishje Els

On day two of the conference, on Thursday afternoon, the lawns of Adelaide University were filled with the sounds of South African song. Busi Nthoba and Lishje Els were facilitating a workshop entitled 'Music: voices of survival' in which they shared their experiences and perspectives of how dancing and singing is therapy. Below, two participants in this workshop - Gloria Marsay and Paul Browde - offer their reflections.

The presentation began with the singing of our national anthem 'Nkosi Sikelela Afrika' (God Bless Africa). We were sitting under one of the most enormous plane trees that I have ever seen, and to begin with there were only a few of us listening. I'm not sure how many, but all the chairs seemed to be occupied. Busi and Lishje began to retell the stories which they had heard. They told us the story of a woman named Adelaide, the story of Patience and Portia, and Moses. They told of struggles, sadness, despair, and they told of the prayerful way in which people sing songs with courage and hope.

What Busi and Lishje did not say in words was conveyed simply in watching them work together. This told a story in itself - a story about people working together, about people of all different colours who have held hands in the past.

Many people who were attending presentations close by were drawn towards this one. The crowd around the tree grew. The atmosphere thickened. When the presentation finally came to an end, the facilitator thanked Lishje and Busi and then provided an opening for those who had been listening to voice their thoughts and feelings. As I looked around, I was amazed at how many people were now present, and how many of them were wiping their eyes. Many people expressed feelings which were obviously overwhelming them.

When I reflect on this experience, I am overwhelmed by it. The spirit of Africa came alive, and I realised how so many of our people draw strength from their God through music and song.[3] At times in my world it seems as if 'negativity' has grown so strong and is so powerful. This writing is a decision to lash out against negativity by documenting some of the 'positivity' of the world. I feel that Lishje and Busi acted as true ambassadors for our country and did a wonderful job of spreading a feeling of hope. They shared with us what an important part music has played, and continues to play, in the process of dealing with oppression and healing.

As I left Adelaide, it was so significant for me to come across these words which were spoken by an Australian singer, Dame Nellie Melba. She said:

My voice has been raised not only in song, but to make the big world outside, through me, understand something of the spirit of my beloved country.

I believe the voices of many South Africans were raised through the voices of Busi and Lishje, and the spirit of our beloved country was brought to the 'big world outside'.

Gloria Marsay[4]

I would love to reflect on the workshop. I want you to know that I was at another workshop and happened to chance upon the last part of yours. I stood there for a while, and realised that I was trying to distance myself a little. However, after a few minutes I found myself completely drawn in. It was the songs ... and the two presenters, two South African women. South Africa, the place where I was born, where I lived till I was twenty-five, and which I left thirteen years ago. It is hard to describe what South Africa means to me. I love the land. I still miss the light, the wind, the rain. The mountains, the sea. I miss the noises, the nights, the stars. Capetown, Table mountain, Rocky street, Crown mines, the game reserve, the evening rains, the hailstorms, the hot summer days, the Jacarandas, the Joburg afternoons ... I miss the people. My family. I miss Africa.

It was in South Africa that I learned to care about people. I learned that people who lived just down the road from me were cold, and hungry, while I lived the life of a king. I learned that my struggles were less important than the struggles of my neighbours. I was taught that some people are more important than others, and that it's okay to discriminate. I was also taught by my parents that people are people, and that justice and freedom are worth living for, even dying for.

Living there, and living with South Africa in my heart, is a great honour and privilege, and also a pain. It was a place of horror, as well as a place in which good triumphed over evil. These are the thoughts that engulf me as I think of that place.

So there I was in Adelaide. Also in the Southern Hemisphere ... and I heard those songs. Those familiar sounds that called to me across the lawns ... and I went there ... and I was transported, back in time, across the oceans, there ... to that place I love ... that is why I cried, and through those songs, South Africa will be part of me, always. Thank you.

Paul Browde

Notes

1. Gloria can be contacted c/- 58 Bompas Rd, Dunkeld 2196, Johannesburg, South Africa, phone/fax: (11) 880 3554.

2. Paul can be contacted c/- 700 West End Avenue #15D, New York NY 10025, USA, phone (1-212) 669 9008, email: poebe@banet.net

3. During the conference there were various discussions about spirituality and its influence on people's lives and work. There was a deliberate effort made to acknowledge a range of spiritualities and different understandings.

4. These reflections by Gloria have been edited. If you'd like the longer, unedited version please email to Gloria: marsay@global.co.za

22.

Thoughts and dilemmas

from the
Conference Collective

In preparation for our inaugural conference we talked to as many people as we could about ways of organising conferences and some of the dilemmas and challenges involved. As the year progressed and the conference began to take shape, we published the following reflections on the thinking behind our conference organising (Gecko, 1998 Vol.2). We hoped that this would invite participants into thinking through both our role and their role in creating a context of care and thoughtfulness within the conference.

We have chosen to republish those reflections here as the process leading up to the conference was in many ways as significant as the event itself.

We believe it is our responsibility as the Conference Collective to create an inclusive, thoughtful, creative conference in which there are forums for many sorts of conversations. We believe it is our role to take care of the process, the participants, and the presenters. As such we are trying to do things differently than other conferences we have attended. If you have any ideas as to what might help we'd love to hear from you.

We believe that it is important for people attending the conference to have access to our ideas, dilemmas, learnings and current thinking about a range of

issues concerning the conference. Below you will find our current thinking on:
(i)   Creating a context of care
(ii)   The role of plenaries
(iii)   The conference structure
(iv)   Creating the conference program and presentations
(v)   Consulting with presenters prior to the conference
(vi)   'Paying the rent'

(i)   Creating a context of care

One of the key issues that we have been thinking through recently has been how to create a context of respect and care for the duration of the conference. We'd like to thank Charles Waldegrave and The Family Centre, Lower Hutt, New Zealand, for sharing with us their thoughts on these issues. The following questions are influencing our discussions, many of them have been informed by the thoughtfulness of The Family Centre:

- *How can we create a context within a conference setting in which the voices, experiences and histories of women and people of marginalised cultures are honoured and respected?*

- *How can we ensure that the norms, values, beliefs and ways of being of women and people from marginalised cultures are fairly represented within the process, structures and the distribution of resources of the conference?*

- *What processes need to take place in the planning of the conference so that the voices of people from marginalised cultures and women are honoured from the beginning of the process?*

- *What needs to occur so that the appropriate welcomes, farewells and introductions are built into the conference?*

- *How can we ensure that the influence of marginalised cultures' and women's ways of being are not limited to particular rituals but inform the ways of speaking and relating throughout the three days and the preparation for the conference?*

- *How can we prepare people for the inevitable differences of* perspective when there are people of different cultures talking about the issues that are so significant to them?

- *How can the sharing of sacred stories and the personal experiences of people from marginalised cultures and women be protected from analytical debate, depersonalised ways of speaking?*

- *What processes will we need to ensure that issues of class are reflected upon so that working-class voices, experiences, histories and ways of being are honoured within the conference process?*

- *What processes will we need to ensure that issues of heterosexual dominance are reflected upon so that the voices, experiences, histories and ways of being of gay, lesbian, bisexual, transgender peoples are honoured within the conference process?*

- *What processes will we need to ensure that the experiences and ways of being of young people are honoured, and that space is created for their voices to be heard?*

We are taking these questions seriously, and also really enjoying thinking them through. We'd love to hear from people if they have any ideas, comments, or even further questions. Closer to the time of the conference we will include in the first edition of the conference newspaper the structures and plans that we have made to address these questions - as well as further questions and dilemmas that will have inevitably been raised!

(ii)   The role of plenaries

We have been trying to think through the concept of keynote addresses or plenaries. Bringing the whole conference together for certain events seems quite wonderful. It means that everyone gets a chance to meet up and that there is some common and shared experience for all conference participants, and it can also set a theme for the day.

Traditional keynote or plenary addresses, however, do raise some questions for us that we are trying to think through. It is easy to create a context in which the participants become passive and set apart from the speaker. It can seem a long way from more interactive contexts in which there is a sharing of experience. Yet simply opening plenary sessions up for questions doesn't seem to provide good outcomes either.

We are trying to question the usual process from the perspective of conference organisers, keynote presenters and participants to create a context that frees up all three groups to find creative ways of making it a different experience. Here are our thoughts so far:

Meet the speakers through their writings:

We invite conference participants to 'meet' the keynote speakers well before the conference by reading their writings. So far all the keynote speakers we have asked to present have published with us personal reflections upon their lives, families and work. Through these stories participants will be invited to get to know the speakers well before the conference. Closer to the time of the conference, we will try to facilitate this process through our website.

Meet the speakers in person:

To try to interrupt the one-way flow of information that is usually involved in plenary sessions, we have come up with the idea of asking all plenary speakers to be available after their talks for smaller informal discussions. These discussions would probably take place sitting under a gum tree or in our alternative venue - the marquee on the lawns.

All of the plenary speakers we have invited so far have loved this idea as they too have been aware of the sense of performance and isolation that can accompany traditional ways of presenting.

Care for the speakers:

As organisers we are trying to play our part differently also. Prior to the conference, we are meeting with all plenary speakers to talk through what will make the conference a good experience for them and what sort of support we can offer. This is being a lovely process.

We are also inviting plenary speakers to stay in touch with us as they write their papers so that we can build on a sense of community and belonging over the conference. We are also going to put them in touch with each other. A support person and family members of the plenary speakers will be able to come to the plenary for free.

We hope that these steps will alter the traditional role of 'plenary' presentations at the conference. We are still thinking these issues through and would be more than happy to hear of people's suggestions and/or comments.

(iii) Conference structure

After many conversations with a wide range of people about what they'd like to see in a conference, we have nearly finalised the structure or shape of the conference. We hope to create a number of different forums throughout the three days in which a variety of different sorts of conversations can take place including: keynote addresses, one hour formal workshops, two-and-a-half hour practice-based seminars, small groups under gum trees, evening workshops, and sessions in a large marquee on the lawns.

We have decided to only have three parallel sessions of formal presentations at any one time. Although this reduces the number of formal presentations, we believe it will enable us to take greater care of the process and to ensure that a creative momentum is sustained throughout the day.

The days will be long! They will begin at 8:30 in the morning and presentations will be planned until 9:30pm at night. We are going to strongly encourage participants not to try to attend everything, but to treat the conference as you would a festival - pick and choose the presentations to attend, take breaks, sit outside and talk with newly-met friends and colleagues. We wish to place an equal importance on the formal and informal conversations that will occur over the three days.

(iv) Creating the conference program and presentations

We are still in the process of working out all the presentations and the conference program. We have deliberately tried to do this differently than many other conferences. In the process we have struggled with the following dilemmas:

- *How can we take care to ensure that all participants who attend the conference find every presentation that they go to engaging, accessible and thoughtful?*

- *How can we find a place for everyone who wants to be involved in the conference to share their work and ideas?*

- *How can we ensure that the range, forums and styles of presentations do justice to issues of class, culture, gender, age and sexuality?*

- *How can we invite people into a conference atmosphere that is not about performance, competition or attaining professional status, but instead about being involved in interesting conversations, learning from one another and sharing ideas?*

- *How can we ensure that the conference is a lovely event for presenters and that there is a sense of connectedness between the conference organisers and those presenting at the conference?*

Rather than put out an anonymous call for papers and then be faced with the choice of either accepting or rejecting abstracts from people we may or may not know, we have tried to develop alternative processes.

As this is the inaugural Dulwich Centre Publications' Conference, lots of our authors will be giving formal practice-based presentations. Meanwhile, the keynote addresses each morning, and other presentations in various forums, will be given by people whose voices are not usually represented at mainstream conferences. Because of both of these priorities it means that there are relatively few spaces still available in formal sessions.

However, because of the conference structure briefly outlined above, we have considerable flexibility in relation to making spaces available for people to be able to share their ideas and thoughts without making a formal presentation to over 100 people. We are currently meeting and talking with a wide range of people and are working out what sort of forum they could best contribute to.

We are also gradually asking all those people who have already registered for the conference, what sorts of ideas, stories and experiences of work they wish to either share with others or hear about at the conference. As we do this we are then working out the most appropriate forums in which this can occur. It is an unusual process but so far it seems to be working really well.

We are very excited about the diversity and thoughtfulness of the presentations that we have already finalised. We are also really enjoying speaking with people who are committed to making the conference a wonderful event about the contributions they wish to make. We have been touched by the generosity and enthusiasm that people have already shown and there is still such a long way to go! If you are already registered for the conference and have ideas in relation to what you might contribute to the conference we'd really like to hear from you.

(v) Consulting with presenters prior to the conference

As this is a Dulwich Centre Publications' Conference, we are trying to find ways of working collaboratively with presenters as we do routinely with authors. We are trying to meet up with as many presenters as possible prior to the conference to talk through their ideas about what will make the conference work, their hopes and ideas, as well as any fears they may have about presenting. This is being a lovely process and is really helping us as organisers to come up with ideas as to how to take care of both presenters and participants during the conference.

Where it is appropriate, we are inviting presenters to write a paper prior to the conference. We hope to gather these papers together and publish them in time for the conference or shortly afterwards. We hope that the process of working collaboratively on these papers prior to the conference will build a solid foundation for the conference itself. So far, it's being a fun and creative process!

(vi) 'Paying the rent'

There is a tradition, particularly within women's conferences and events in Australia, of finding ways to financially acknowledge Indigenous

Australians' prior ownership of the land on which the event is to take place. A system of 'paying the rent' has evolved. The histories to this system appear to stem back one hundred and sixty years. In recent years organisers of events have 'paid the rent' directly to the local Indigenous Australian community, or to established Indigenous Australian organisations.

In relation to the conference, the same amount that we will be paying to rent the premises in which the conference is to take place will be put aside. We are still discussing with Indigenous Australians involved in the conference how this 'rent money' will be distributed back to Indigenous Australians.

23.

Ongoing conversations

This is an extract from the post-conference newsheet that was sent out to all participants.

Some very creative and exciting conversations flourished over the time of the conference and we are hoping these will continue and gradually take shape into publications. There are a couple of themes which we at Dulwich Centre have particular energy and commitment towards at this time.

Firstly, we wish to find creative ways of talking and working with troubles in workplaces. This seems to be an issue which many people in the field have struggled with and one that we are currently grappling with. We would have really valued being able to read thoughtful discussions on this topic but were unable to find any that were helpful.

Now, we are looking at publishing some papers around these issues. At the conference, Maggie Carey facilitated a session around addressing troubles in therapy networks. Next year we'd like there to be a session at the conference on addressing troubles in workplaces. We'd love to hear from people about their stories around these issues - stories of good resolutions, dilemmas that people have struggled with, ways of leaving well, successful rituals of transition, etc.

Secondly, a theme that emerged from discussions at the conference was the link between our work practices and spirituality. How do our spiritual beliefs and practices inform our work and vice-versa? How can we work creatively and respectfully in relation to other people's spiritual beliefs? What possibilities do considerations of spiritual beliefs and traditions open up? What possibilities would be opened up if we found ways of speaking together about these issues across different cultural/spiritual beliefs and traditions?

Thirdly, a further theme that emerged from conversations at the conference involved illness narratives. What are the narratives that inform our understandings and experiences of illness? What are the political and practical implications of these narratives? When particular illnesses are imbued with social stigma and discrimination how do people resist invitations of shame and isolation? What are the dilemmas associated with speaking about issues of illness? Whose stories are they to tell?

We hope that over the course of this year publications will take shape around these themes. If people are interested in contributing ideas around these topics please write to David Denborough c/- Dulwich Centre Publications. The conference was so filled with rich conversations that it is exciting to think of these continuing into the written word.

Appendix
Related reading

A number of presentations that were given at the conference have been recently published elsewhere, or are soon to be published. We thought some readers might be interested in a list of where they could follow these up. Here are the references.

Day One

Maggie Carey, 1998: 'Communities of shared experience, from an interview with Maggie Carey.' *Gecko*, Vol.1.

Barb Wingard, 1996: 'Introducing sugar.' In 'A spirit on its own is easily broken but together we will not break', *Dulwich Centre Newsletter*, No.3.

Barb Wingard, 1996: 'Grief: Remember, reflect, reveal.' In 'A spirit on its own is easily broken but together we will not break', *Dulwich Centre Newsletter*, No.3.

Multicultural narrative team, 1998: 'Creating respectful relationships in the name of the Latino family: A community approach to domestic violence', Part One, *Dulwich Centre Newsletter*, No.1.

Yvonne Sliep & the CARE Counsellors, Malawi, 1996: 'A spirit on its own is easily broken but together we will not break', Part One, *Dulwich Centre Newsletter*, No.3.

Day Two

Cecily Nichols, 1998: 'A story of survival.' In 'Taking the hassle out of school and stories from younger people', *Dulwich Centre Journal*, Nos.2&3.

Ashley Couzens, 'Sharing the load: Group conversations with young Indigenous men.' *Gecko*, Vol.3.

Loretta Perry, 1999: '*Mitakuyu Oyasin:* All of my relations: Exploring metaphors of connectedness.' In Morgan, A. (ed), *Once Upon a Time: Narrative therapy with children and their families,* Chapter 8. Adelaide: Dulwich Centre Publications.

Silent Too Long, 1998: 'Your voices inspire mine.' In 'Some thoughtful considerations in relation to working on issues of violence and abuse', *Dulwich Centre Journal*, No.4.

Patrick O'Leary, 1998: 'Liberation from self-blame: Working with men who have experienced childhood sexual abuse.' In 'Some thoughtful considerations in relation to working on issues of violence and abuse', *Dulwich Centre Journal*, No.4.

'Taking the hassle out of school and stories from younger people', 1998: *Dulwich Centre Journal*, Nos.2&3.

Alice Morgan, 1999: 'Once upon a time ...' In Morgan, A. (ed), *Once Upon a Time: Narrative therapy with children and their families,* Chapter 1. Adelaide: Dulwich Centre Publications.

Jane Waldegrave, 1999: 'Towards "settled stories": Working with children when a child or parent dies in a family.' In Morgan, A. (ed), *Once Upon a Time: Narrative therapy with children and their families,* Chapter 10. Adelaide: Dulwich Centre Publications.

Vicki Dickerson, 1998: 'Silencing critical voices. An interview with Marie-Nathalie Beaudoin.' *Gecko*, Vol.2.

Mark Trudinger, Cameron Boyd & Peter Melrose, 1998: 'Questioning sexuality: A workshop in progress.' In 'Some thoughtful considerations in relation to working on issues of violence and abuse', *Dulwich Centre Journal*, No.4.

Jesus Tovar, 1998: 'Reclaiming culture and community.' In 'Taking the hassle out of school and stories from younger people', *Dulwich Centre Journal*, Nos.2&3.

Ruth Orchison, 1997: 'From pain-full narratives to pain-less lives.' In 'Challenging disabling practices: Talking about issues of disability', *Dulwich Centre Newsletter*, No.4.

Jen Williamson, Anna Williamson & Jasmine Jones, 1997: 'Women's ways and intellectual disability.' In 'Challenging disabling practices: Talking about issues of disability', *Dulwich Centre Newsletter*, No.4.

Lorna Roberts, Bernie Francis & Vi Eastham, 1999: 'Forever able.' *Gecko*, Vol.1

Day Three

Chris Burke, 1998: 'Working with the interface of domestic violence and child protection.' In 'Some thoughtful considerations in relation to working on issues of violence and abuse', *Dulwich Centre Journal*, No.4.

Sophin Kheav & Chak-Riya Engelhardt, 1998: 'Talking about domestic violence in the Cambodian community.' In 'Some thoughtful considerations in relation to working on issues of violence and abuse', *Dulwich Centre Journal*, No.4.

Maxine Joy, 1999: 'Shame on who? Consulting with children who have experienced sexual abuse.' In Morgan, A. (ed), *Once Upon a Time: Narrative therapy with children and their families,* Chapter 9. Adelaide: Dulwich Centre Publications.

Kiwi Tamasese, Charles Waldegrave, Flora Tuhaka & Warihi Campbell, 1998: 'Furthering conversation about partnerships of accountability.' In 'Some thoughtful considerations in relation to working on issues of violence and abuse', *Dulwich Centre Journal*, No.4.

Upcoming

Jonathan Morgan, 1999: 'The Great African Homeless Writers' Project.' To be published in an upcoming issue on Homelessness in the *Dulwich Centre Journal.*

'Keeping Ubuntu alive: Caring for people and community.' To be published in an upcoming issue of *Gecko.*

'Healing in Unity: Reflections from the Bowraville Gathering.' A full write-up of the Bowraville Gathering will be published later this year. Contact Dulwich Centre for details.

'Farewell from Adelaide'

(song)

farewell from Adelaide
from this conference gathering
that's gone on for days and days
if you're now leaving Australia
well goodbye - I mean see ya later
oh won't you please remember
you're welcome back any day

there've been an awful lot of conversations
between peoples of many nations
I can still hear the singing, the dancing, the didges on the lawns
can still see our young people proudly sharing stories of their own

and now as you travel on home
with new stories to share quietly with your own
please arrive in good shape
that way your loved ones will know that
entrusting you to us was no mistake

farewell from Adelaide
from this conference gathering
that's gone on for days and days
if you're now leaving Australia
well goodbye - I mean see ya later
oh won't you please remember
you're welcome back any day
we hope you found what you came for
from skills-based workshops
to meeting friends from afar
we're so glad you came
next year if all goes well
perhaps we'll see you here again

Farewell

from

Lewis O'Brien

Senior Elder of the Kaurna People

Ngai Kundo punggorendi na kurlangga.
Natta padninga   *Kouandaku*
       Meriku
       Patpanna
       Wonggaku
Ngai yaintya tikkota.
       Nakkota.

I'll feel the pain of you all leaving.
Now you all go to the North
       East
       South
       West.
I'll remain here.
       See you.

Now turn and hug the person next to you.

Narrative Therapy and Community Work Conference

Adelaide 2000
February 16th-18th

We are excited to let you know that the second Dulwich Centre Publications' *Narrative Therapy and Community Work Conference* is to be held in Adelaide, South Australia, from 16th-18th February 2000. Seeing as there was such a good response to our inaugural conference, we're doing it again. The conference is to be surrounded by a week of events - ranging from a women's gathering, workshops, to our own mini-festival!

The Conference aims to gather together practitioners from a wide range of backgrounds and experiences who are involved in exciting and hopeful work informed by narrative ideas and practices. Many of the structures will be similar to those of our inaugural conference - we will try to create a number of different forums throughout the three days in which a variety of different sorts of conversations can take place. These will include: keynote addresses, two and a half hour practice-based seminars; one hour formal workshops; small group discussions under gum trees and umbrellas; evening workshops; and sessions in a large Marquee on the lawns. On the Thursday evening there will be a picnic dinner and concert.

For a full brochure about the conference, the workshops and extra events that we are organising, please contact:

Dulwich Centre Publications
Hutt St PO Box 7192
Adelaide 5000
phone (61-8) 8223 3966
fax (61-8) 08 8232 4441